Family Firms into International Markets

Claudia Pongelli

Family Firms into International Markets

Research Trajectories and Empirical Insights on Entry Mode Decisions

palgrave
macmillan

Claudia Pongelli
Department of Management and Law
University of Rome Tor Vergata
Rome, Italy

This book has been externally peer reviewed in accordance with Palgrave Macmillan's our peer review policy, which can be found here: https://www.springernature.com/gp/policies/book-publishing-policies

ISBN 978-3-031-05397-9 ISBN 978-3-031-05398-6 (eBook)
https://doi.org/10.1007/978-3-031-05398-6

This Palgrave Macmillan imprint is published by the registered company Springer Nature Switzerland AG.
The registered company address is: Gewerbestrasse 11, 6330 Cham, Switzerland

To Marco,
wonderful husband, amazing father,
and extraordinary leader of a family business.

Acknowledgments

This book reflects a ten-year research journey at the interface between the family business and the international business fields. Along this exciting path, a number of key relationships with national and international scholars have enriched my knowledge and contributed to the growth of my research. I wish to express my sincere gratitude to all of them. Moreover, parts of this book come from my Ph.D thesis and have been presented to several seminars and conferences, such as, Academy of Management (AOM), EURAM (European Academy of Management) and IFERA (International Family Enterprise Research Academy), among others. I am grateful to all in the audience who supplied constructive feedbacks, and thereby aiding to progress my research forwards.

Contents

1 An Introduction to International Entry Modes Decisions in Family Firms 1

2 Family Firms and International Entry Modes: A State-Of-The-Art 9

3 The Choice Between Wholly Owned Subsidiaries and Joint Ventures Within Family Firms: A Theoretical Investigation from the Socioemotional Wealth Perspective 35

4 The Choice Between Wholly-Owned Subsidiaries and Joint Ventures Within Family Firms: An Empirical Analysis 55

Index 87

List of Figures

Fig. 2.1	An integrative framework on entry mode choices. (Adapted from Pan & Tse, 2000)	10
Fig. 4.1	Results of the analyses	81

List of Tables

Table 4.1	Foreign entries statistics and geographic distribution	62
Table 4.2	Descriptive statistics	64
Table 4.3	Wholly-owned subsidiary propensity for family and non-family led firms	65
Table 4.4	Probit models. Dependent variable: WOS. Sample: Full, Low performance hazard and High performance hazard	68
Table 4.5	Average marginal effects. Dependent variable: WOS. Sample: Full, Low performance hazard and High performance hazard	69
Table 4.6	Probit models. Dependent variable: WOS. Sample: High emotional hazard and Low emotional hazard	70
Table 4.7	Average marginal effects. Dependent variable: WOS. Sample: High emotional hazard and Low emotional hazard	71
Table 4.8	Probit models. Dependent variable: WOS. Sample: Combinations of performance hazard and emotional hazard	72
Table 4.9	Average marginal effects. Dependent variable: WOS. Sample: Combinations of performance hazard and emotional hazard	74

CHAPTER 1

An Introduction to International Entry Modes Decisions in Family Firms

Abstract The first chapter of this book introduces the family firms internationalization as a growing and multifaced field of inquiry. It is explained why this area of research is attracting growing scholarly attention and how it has been evolving over the year. Then the specific focus on entry modes and its relevance is presented and the structure of the book is outlined.

Keywords Family firms • Internationalization • Entry modes

Family firms are defined as "*organizations in which families exercise substantial influence on the firm's affairs*" (Gomez-Mejia et al., 2011, p. 660). They represent more than 80% of all firms in most of countries (La Porta et al., 1999) and on average have higher growth rates around the world than non-family firms (Miroshnychenko et al., 2021). Given that the importance of family firms in developed and emerging markets as well as among top MNEs is progressively growing (Carr & Bateman, 2009), their international processes and strategies have been attracting growing scholarly attention over the last three decades. As a result, family firms'

The author is also Affiliate Researcher at IPAG Entrepreneurship & Family Business Center, IPAG Business School, France.

C. Pongelli, *Family Firms into International Markets*,
https://doi.org/10.1007/978-3-031-05398-6_1

internationalization has been intensively investigated through a variety of theoretical lenses, empirical methods, and context of analyses by scholars from different fields and theoretical traditions. Such a high interest is motivated by the presence of some distinctive aspects in family firms which are due to the involvement of family members at different levels of the governance structure of the firm and have a strong influence over their international choices and outcomes. Indeed, the intertwinement between the family and the business, which uniquely characterize family firms, leads to an unparalleled coexistence of economic and non-economic goals as drivers of international behaviors.

For example, in 2013, Kassatly Chtaura a second-generation Lebanon-based family company producing both alcoholic and non-alcoholic beverages, gave up on establishing a subsidiary in Saudi Arabia despite the strategic attractiveness of the move: due to its family business nature, the firm was not suitable for internationalization. Indeed, the firm's main managerial roles were all in the hands of the three owning siblings and none of these family members were prone to leave Lebanon and relocate abroad in order to directly control foreign operations neither resolute enough to go against the father's dream to diversify the business in the home country rather than venturing internationally (Schaan & Fathallah, 2015). In a similar vein, Kano and Verbeke (2018) reported the example of Tavazo Iran, a third-generation Tehran-based family company producing dried fruit, which chose Canada for its first international subsidiary because of the appealing quality of life for the owning family promised by this location (e.g. stable political environment; good education for children; immigration program to facilitate family members relocation), compared to other attractive countries.

More in general, the willingness to keep family control over international operations and satisfy the owning family needs, the wish to provide job opportunities to family members through international activities, the long term horizon of international investments to foster the transgenerational continuity of the business and the natural tendency to play safe on international markets to safeguard family harmony are just some of the family-related distinctive goals that previous studies found to have both positive and negative influence over the international efforts made by family firms (Pongelli et al., 2021b).

With the aim to produce integrated knowledge in this field of inquiry, in recent years several scholars embarked on the effort to systematize this body of literature. The importance of this goal was first intuited by

Kontinen and Ojala (2010) with an initial review of studies on the internationalization of family firms. However, in 2010 only 25 studies were produced on this topic and the scholarly knowledge was still very limited. Yet, given the rapid rise of this area of research, only a few years later Pukall and Calabrò (2014) published their systematic review on 72 journal articles with the aim to help this field of inquiry to produce consistent results, gain legitimacy and grow. Indeed, they observed that previous findings were highly disjunctive and to overcome this inconclusiveness, they integrated international business and family business theoretical approaches to propose a revised version of the traditional Uppsala Model[1] inspired by Socioemotional Wealth[2] underpinnings to explain the role of risk preferences, knowledge, and network ties for family firms' internationalization. Subsequently, Arregle et al. (2017) proposed a meta-analysis of 76 studies across 41 countries to understand the impact of family control on the scale and scope of internationalization, along with the moderating role of institutions. More recently, using a rigorous bibliometric approach, the review by Casprini and her team attests "*the emancipation of family firm internationalization as a distinct and yet highly heterogeneous field of research*" and pinpoints ownership, diversification decisions, networks and international entrepreneurial orientation as major ongoing research themes (Casprini et al., 2020, p. 2). Furthermore, according to Debellis et al. (2021) the evolution of this stream of literature over the three past decades went through different waves of studies characterized not only by different time periods but also by distinctive research questions and topics. They recognize in the first wave of research on family firms' internationalization the common aim to understand differences between family and non-family firms; instead, subsequent waves were devoting more and more attention to family firms' heterogeneity

[1] The Upsala model was first developed in 1977 and subsequently revised and integrated from different perspectives to offer a dynamic and process-based explanation to internationalization. This theory is usually employed to explain firms internationalization as a process of gradual commitment in foreign markets (Johanson & Vahlne, 1977; Vahlne & Johanson, 2017).

[2] Socioemotional Wealth is a widely employed theoretical approach born in the family business field to explain the risk preferences of family principals. According to the Socioemotional Wealth theoretical perspective, family principals prefer strategic alternatives which allow the preservation of the socioemotional endowment of the owning family i.e., "the non-financial aspects of the firm that meet the family's affective needs, such as identity, the ability to exercise family influence, and the perpetuity of the family dynasty" (Gómez-Mejía et al., 2007, p. 106).

along with the attempt to grasp family firms' characteristics which lead these firms to adopt heterogenous behaviors into international markets. Moreover, according to their review on 134 articles from the infancy of this literature to more recent times, research moved from considering export as the only dimension of internationalization for family firms to more sophisticated forms of foreign markets entry modes (Debellis et al., 2021). This also corresponded to a change of focus from the "*what*" to the "*how*" research question: while initial studies were mainly concerned to understand which factors make family firms more or less international, the scholarly attention has now switched to a more accurate assessment on how family firms makes decisions related to the different types of entry modes.

Moreover, a new challenge is emerging in this field with respect to the need to bridge better the international business and the family business domain. This issue was first addressed by Casillas and Moreno-Menéndez (2017) who offered a review of prior studies with the aim to identify common patterns in this stream of studies as well as the potential area of dialogue between the disciplines of family business and international business. In the same line, Arregle et al. (2021) noted that all the above mentioned reviews are mainly oriented to address the needs of a family business audience and fail to provide an assessment of these studies from the international business perspective. To fill this gap, they provide a major effort of review of 220 contribution and unpack this body of research along seven core international business themes, including international entry modes among them (Arregle et al., 2021).

Entry mode decisions are recognized as one of the most critical step in the internationalization process (Anderson & Gatignon, 1986; Hennart & Slangen, 2014) for their strong implications on organizational control over foreign operations, investment risk involved, resource commitment and firm performance (Brouthers, 2002). They can be defined as "*structural agreements that allow a firm to implement its product market strategy in a host country either by carrying out only the market operations (export), or both production and marketing operations there by itself or in partnership with others (contractual modes, joint ventures, wholly owned operations)*" (Sharma & Erramilli, 2004, p. 4).

For family firms the choice among different entry modes has an additional meaning as family members are emotionally bounded to the firm and the strategic decisions about entering foreign target markets also rely on family-related considerations strongly (e.g. Kano & Verbeke, 2018; Pongelli et al., 2016, 2021a).

Although a default preference for a given entry mode is not always predictable due to the occurrence of internal and contextual factors (Arregle et al., 2021), family decision-makers are deemed to adopt entry mode strategies that minimize various risks, especially with respect to the risk of dissipating their socioemotional endowment (Gómez-Mejía et al., 2007, 2010). The actual emphasis family firms place over this risk-reduction approach and their distinctive family-related goals leads them to behave differently from non-family firms in their international endeavors as well as to generate heterogenous behaviors across family firms with different characteristics.

The aim of this book is to improve the understanding of entry mode decisions in family firms, firstly by offering an integrated discussion of extant literature, and secondly providing theoretical and empirical insights on the different drivers which influence family leaders strategic international preferences with respect to one of the most important entry mode choices i.e. the choice between either creating a joint venture or a wholly-owned subsidiary in a foreign country (Erramilli, 1996; Makino & Neupert, 2000).

More precisely, this book is organized as follows. To get a better understanding of the state of the art in this crowded but fragmented stream of literature, a full description of the literature background is provided and the different types of entry modes are explained in detail in Chap. 2. Specifically, previous studies within the family business field are grouped according to the two main categories of entry modes, i.e., equity and non-equity. Within each category, previous studies are further classified and described according to the specific type of entry mode (or entry mode decision) they investigated. For each type of entry mode, common patterns and main research trajectories are outlined.

Then, Chap. 3 introduces a theoretical investigation based on the Socioemotional Wealth (SEW) approach and discusses how the reluctance to lose family control—as one of the main dimensions of SEW—influence family leaders in their subsidiary ownership choices. Specifically, this chapter develops a conceptual argumentation about the role that performance and emotional hazards as well as the cultural distance between the domestic and the foreign country have in shaping family leaders' international risk preferences with respect to choice between wholly-owned subsidiary and joint venture.

Finally, Chap. 4 offers an empirical validation of the theoretical propositions developed in the previous chapter. In more detail, based on a sample of 3939 foreign subsidiaries run by 586 family-controlled firms, it provides empirical evidence about the trade-offs and interactions between performance and emotional hazards as drivers of the choice between wholly-owned subsidiary and joint venture in family led firms and also addresses the moderating role of cultural distance. Results of the analyses show that depending on whether firm performance is improving or declining, the family leader is—respectively—more or less driven by the desire to preserve family control when making international strategic decisions and, therefore, more or less likely to enter a foreign market through a wholly-owned subsidiary. Findings also suggest that this tendency is either weakened or amplified by the level of the emotional hazard, indicating that when low performance hazard matches with high emotional hazard the family leader's willingness to preserve family control trough a wholly-owned subsidiary is stronger. Moreover, we show that the impact of emotional hazard on family leader's choice about the subsidiary ownership policy weakens as the cultural distance between the domestic and the foreign country increases.

References

Anderson, E., & Gatignon, H. (1986). Modes of foreign entry: A transaction cost analysis and propositions. *Journal of International Business Studies, 17*(3), 1–26. https://doi.org/10.1057/palgrave.jibs.8490432

Arregle, J. L., Duran, P., Hitt, M. A., & van Essen, M. (2017). Why is family firms' internationalization unique? A meta-analysis. *Entrepreneurship Theory and Practice, 41*(5), 801–831. https://doi.org/10.1111/etap.12246

Arregle, J. L., Chirico, F., Kano, L., Kundu, S. K., Majocchi, A., & Schulze, W. S. (2021). Family firm internationalization: Past research and an agenda for the future. *Journal of International Business Studies, 52*(6), 1159–1198. https://doi.org/10.1057/s41267-021-00425-2

Brouthers, K. D. (2002). Institutional, cultural and transaction cost influences on entry mode choice and performance. *Journal of International Business Studies, 33*(2), 203–221. https://doi.org/10.1057/palgrave.jibs.8491013

Carr, C., & Bateman, S. (2009). International strategy configurations of the world's top family firms. *Management International Review, 49*(6), 733–758. https://doi.org/10.1007/s11575-009-0018-3

Casillas, J. C., & Moreno-Menéndez, A. M. (2017). International business and family business: Potential dialogue between disciplines. *European Journal of Family Business, 7*(1–2), 25–40. https://doi.org/10.1016/j.ejfb.2017.08.001

Casprini, E., Dabic, M., Kotlar, J., & Pucci, T. (2020). A bibliometric analysis of family firm internationalization research: Current themes, theoretical roots, and ways forward. *International Business Review, 29*(5), 101715. https://doi.org/10.1016/j.ibusrev.2020.101715

Debellis, F., Rondi, E., Plakoyiannaki, E., & De Massis, A. (2021). Riding the waves of family firm internationalization: A systematic literature review, integrative framework, and research agenda. *Journal of World Business, 56*(1), 101144. https://doi.org/10.1016/j.jwb.2020.101144

Erramilli, M. K. (1996). Nationality and subsidiary ownership patterns in multinational corporations. *Journal of International Business Studies, 27*(2), 225–248. https://doi.org/10.1057/palgrave.jibs.8490133

Gómez-Mejía, L. R., Haynes, K. T., Núñez-Nickel, M., Jacobson, K. J., & Moyano-Fuentes, J. (2007). Socioemotional wealth and business risks in family-controlled firms: Evidence from Spanish olive oil mills. *Administrative Science Quarterly, 52*(1), 106–137. https://doi.org/10.2189/asqu.52.1.106

Gomez-Mejia, L. R., Makri, M., & Larraza Kintana, M. (2010). Diversification decisions in family-controlled firms. *Journal of Management Studies, 47*(2), 223–252. https://doi.org/10.1111/j.1467-6486.2009.00889.x

Gomez-Mejia, L. R., Cruz, C., Berrone, P., & De Castro, J. (2011). The bind that ties: Socioemotional wealth preservation in family firms. *Academy of Management Annals, 5*(1), 653–707. https://doi.org/10.5465/19416520.2011.593320

Hennart, J. F., & Slangen, A. H. (2014). Yes, we really do need more entry mode studies! A commentary on Shaver. *Journal of International Business Studies, 46*(1), 114–122. https://doi.org/10.1057/jibs.2014.39

Johanson, J., & Vahlne, J. E. (1977). The internationalization process of the firm – A model of knowledge development and increasing foreign market commitments. *Journal of International Business Studies, 8*(1), 23–32. https://doi.org/10.1057/palgrave.jibs.8490676

Kano, L., & Verbeke, A. (2018). Family firm internationalization: Heritage assets and the impact of bifurcation bias. *Global Strategy Journal, 8*(1), 158–183. https://doi.org/10.1002/gsj.1186

Kontinen, T., & Ojala, A. (2010). The internationalization of family businesses: A review of extant research. *Journal of Family Business Strategy, 1*(2), 97–107. https://doi.org/10.1016/j.jfbs.2010.04.001

Kontinen, T., & Ojala, A. (2012). Internationalization pathways among family-owned SMEs. *International Marketing Review, 29*(5), 496–518. https://doi.org/10.1108/02651331211260359

La Porta, R., Lopez-de-Silanes, F., & Shleifer, A. (1999). Corporate ownership around the world. *The Journal of Finance, 54*(2), 471–517. https://doi.org/10.1111/0022-1082.00115

Makino, S., & Neupert, K. E. (2000). National culture, transaction costs, and the choice between joint venture and wholly owned subsidiary. *Journal of International Business Studies, 31*(4), 705–713. https://doi.org/10.1057/palgrave.jibs.8490930

Miroshnychenko, I., De Massis, A., Miller, D., & Barontini, R. (2021). Family business growth around the world. *Entrepreneurship Theory and Practice, 45*(4), 682–708. https://doi.org/10.1177/1042258720913028

Pongelli, C., Caroli, M. G., & Cucculelli, M. (2016). Family business going abroad: The effect of family ownership on foreign market entry mode decisions. *Small Business Economics, 47*(3), 787–801. https://doi.org/10.1007/s11187-016-9763-4

Pongelli, C., Calabrò, A., Quarato, F., Minichilli, A., & Corbetta, G. (2021a). Out of the comfort zone! Family leaders' subsidiary ownership choices and the role of vulnerabilities. *Family Business Review, 34*(4), 404–424. https://doi.org/10.1177/08944865211050858

Pongelli, C., Valentino, A., Calabrò, A., & Caroli, M. G. (2021b). Family-centered goals, geographic focus and family firms' internationalization: A study on export performance. *Entrepreneurship & Regional Development, 33*(7–8), 580–598. https://doi.org/10.1080/08985626.2021.1925851

Pukall, T. J., & Calabrò, A. (2014). The internationalization of family firms: A critical review and integrative model. *Family Business Review, 27*(2), 103–125. https://doi.org/10.1177/0894486513491423

Schaan, J. L., & Fathallah, R. (2015). Kassatly Chtaura: Time to expand abroad? *Harvard Business Case*, Ivey Publishing, pp. 1–13.

Sharma, V. M., & Erramilli, M. K. (2004). Resource-based explanation of entry mode choice. *Journal of Marketing Theory and Practice, 12*(1), 1–18. https://doi.org/10.1080/10696679.2004.11658509

Vahlne, J. E., & Johanson, J. (2017). From internationalization to evolution: The Uppsala model at 40 years. *Journal of International Business Studies, 48*(9), 1087–1102. https://doi.org/10.1057/s41267-017-0107-7

CHAPTER 2

Family Firms and International Entry Modes: A State-Of-The-Art

Abstract This chapter offers an integrated discussion on the different types of entry modes adopted by family firms. Specifically, with the aim to map the extant literature on this theme, for each type of entry mode a detailed description of main scholarly contributions produced so far in the family business field is provided. Common topics, major literature trajectories and valuable empirical findings are reported. Moreover, special attention is devoted to outline differences both between family and non-family firms as well as within the heterogeneous universe of family firms.

Keywords Family firms • Entry modes • Export • Joint ventures • FDIs • Subsidiaries

2.1 The Different Types of Entry Modes

In their international strategy, firms can choose among a wide array of different entry modes to enter a foreign market. Although not always unilaterally determined by the firm, entry mode decisions represent one of the most critical choices in the internationalization process (Anderson & Gatignon, 1986; Brouthers & Hennart, 2007; Hennart & Slangen,

The author is also Affiliate Researcher at IPAG Entrepreneurship & Family Business Center, IPAG Business School, France.

C. Pongelli, *Family Firms into International Markets*,
https://doi.org/10.1007/978-3-031-05398-6_2

2014). They can be distinguished into two main categories, i.e. equity and non-equity modes. In the first case, the firm creates an independent organization in the foreign country, alone in the case of a wholly-owned subsidiary or in cooperation with another firm in case of a joint venture; (in the second case, the foreign entry does not imply an equity-based investment, and internationalization usually takes the form of either export or contractual agreements with external parties (such as, for example, franchising or licensing)). Evidently, this choice reflects a different time horizon of the investment and its returns: while equity modes embody a major and long-term oriented resource commitment in the foreign market, non-equity modes are usually easier to exit and investment and returns are specified in advance in a contract (Anderson & Gatignon, 1986; Pan & Tse, 2000). In Fig. 2.1, a summary of the main types of entry modes is provided. To get a better understanding of this area of research in the family business context and drawing inspiration from the hierarchical model on entry mode decisions (Pan & Tse, 2000) this chapter describes and groups previous studies on family firms' entry modes according to the main types of entry modes proposed in this framework. Previous studies are classified according to the two main categories of entry modes, i.e. equity and non-equity in more detail. Within each category, previous

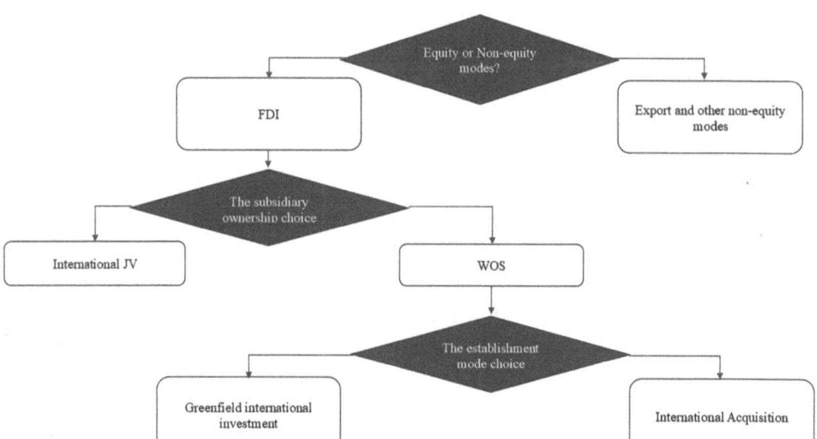

Fig. 2.1 An integrative framework on entry mode choices. (Adapted from Pan & Tse, 2000)

studies are further distinguished according to the specific type of entry mode (or entry mode decision) that they investigated.

However, for the sake of completeness, not all previous studies could be assigned to these categories. Indeed, some articles have a broader scope of analysis and their contribution cannot be limited to one type of entry mode only. Firstly, in this group are included some exploratory qualitative studies which describe the internationalization of family firms from a process-based perspective (Calabrò et al., 2016; Cano-Rubio et al., 2021; Colli et al., 2013; Kontinen & Ojala, 2012). While the majority of previous studies on family firms and entry modes adopt quantitative methods, there are also some interesting qualitative efforts which provide a first understanding on the different entry modes adopted along this process and their evolution over time. Kontinen and Ojala (2012), for example, show that family SMEs can pursue different internationalization pathways spanning from a traditional process—where export is the starting point and foreign subsidiaries are settled only after a long international experience—to born global or born again global forms of internationalization—where the firm establishes foreign subsidiaries from the beginning of its internationalization. In a similar vein, Calabrò et al. (2016) identify four patterns of internationalization which entail a different use of entry modes: the conflicting internationalization; the born global; the direct exporter; and the international founder-managed. Another interesting example is the recent qualitative study developed by Cano-Rubio et al. (2021) on Spanish firms which investigates the influence of familiness (i.e. the specific bundle of capabilities and resources resulting from the involvement of a family in the business) over internationalization. Their findings indicate that export still represents the most commonly used international market entry mode among family firms and that foreign direct investments are adopted only by those firms with a strong familiness. More specifically, their foreign direct investments often consist in either 50% joint venture or the establishment of local sales office that could boost sales in international market.

Secondly, there are also studies which propose a sequential approach to entry modes, thus addressing more entry modes in a single study. Those studies suggest that the entry mode decision is the product of a sequential process. Although sometimes characterized by a fast succession of stages, this process splits the entry mode complex decision into a hierarchical selection process, making the decision less complex. Specifically, Pongelli et al. (2016) decouple the entry mode decisions into two interconnected steps: the first step is the choice between either equity or non-equity mode; the second step is the choice within the entry mode selected at the first step: between contractual agreement and export (non-equity mode) or between joint venture and wholly-owned subsidiary (equity mode). This study shows how different types of family owners (i.e. founder, multiple family members, multiple nuclear families) prefer different entry modes as these modes are differently related to the time horizon of the investment and the cooperation with external actors, both aspects strongly connected to the preservation of their socioemotional endowment. With a similar logic, Xu et al. (2020) proposed a two-stage sequential approach in investigating the subsidiary ownership choice and the establishment mode.

In the subsequent sections, each type of entry mode is described in detail. According to the different types of entry modes, differences between family and non-family firms as well as sources of heterogeneity across family firms are pointed out.

2.2 Family Firms and Non-equity Entry Modes

Export

Export refers to products or services that are produced or manufactured in one country and sold in another. Thus, this entry mode takes the form of international sales which can be executed either by the firm independently (i.e. direct export) or through the cooperation of intermediaries (i.e. indirect export). Despite the increasing complexity characterizing international strategies nowadays, exporting is still seen as a viable option to enter foreign markets, especially in industries in which business models force production in the specific world regions for efficiency reasons, making exporting the only feasible option. Thus, thinking of exporting as an old-fashioned or simply "*easy way*" for firms to approach international markets is sometimes inaccurate. As a consequence, for scholars it is of pivotal importance to know which factors boost international sales and therefore lead to a higher export performance (Chen et al., 2016).

A number of studies in the family business field tried to provide a solid answer to the question of which corporate governance characteristics within family firms improve export intensity. Starting from the explorative study on family firms' internationalization by Zahra (2003), who provided evidence on a sample of 409 U.S. manufacturing firms that family ownership and family involvement in the management are positively associated with international sales, several other studies expanded this initial contribution later on. Cho and Lee (2017) showed that Korean SMEs with high family ownership accumulate strategic capabilities and resources and exploit agency benefits that sustain export performance. Zhou et al. (2019) argued that family ownership is a special resource that can supply family firms with a unique family human capital, social capital, patient capital and survivability capital, and all these resources are beneficial for export depth and breadth. Instead, Fernandez and Nieto (2005, 2006) found evidence in the opposite direction and showed that family ownership has a negative impact on export. According to the authors, family ownership represents an obstacle to build the strategic resources needed to succeed in foreign markets; additionally, conflicts of interests between family and business and the difficulties in obtaining financial resources as well as accumulating intangible resources also hinder export performance. A similar finding has been recently provided by Yang et al. (2020) in the context of Chinese family SMEs. Under the theoretical lens of socioemotional wealth theory (SEW) this study found that higher levels of family ownership reduce export activities within family firms, especially with respect to the initial decision to internationalize (i.e. export propensity) as this decision is perceived as particularly threatening the socioemotional endowment of the owning family.

In the attempt to provide a reasonable explanation for prior conflictive evidence, Sciascia et al. (2012) suggested a non-linear relationship between family ownership and international intensity (i.e. the percentage of sales generated from international markets) as well its scope (i.e. the number of different countries in which the company does business). Their study found empirical support for a U-shaped relationship according to export activities are maximized when ownership stays at moderate levels. In so doing, they reconcile the conflicting results of Zahra (2003) and Fernandez and Nieto (2006) regarding the positive or the negative effects of family ownership on internationalization and indicate that: "*when family ownership becomes excessive, negative effects predicted by stagnation in terms of reduced resource base, risk-aversion, and conflicts among family members reduce the positive effects of family ownership predicted by stewardship*" (Sciascia et al., 2012, p. 22). This insight has been recently integrated by Pascucci et al. (2021) who also proposed a U-shaped relationship but also showed that the highest levels of export performance correspond not only to the lowest but also to the highest family ownership levels. Indeed, according to their opinion, a blend of family and non-family ownership leads to a lower performance because of the presence of conflicting voices dominating strategic visions which could harm the firm's export commitment. Their study highlighted the importance of considering also the moderating role of the financial dimensions, especially for family SMEs whose financial restrictions may impede or make it especially hard for international sales (Pascucci et al., 2021).

Another insightful explanation for prior mixed findings is provided by moving from a static to a dynamic perspective on the relationship between family control and export. The study by Monreal-Pérez and Sánchez-Marín (2017) relied on a Spanish sample of 225 family firms switching to non-family control during the period 2006–2012 and matched them with a control sample of over 4213 family firms remaining under family control. This study showed that transitioning from family control to non-family control worsens the firm's export activity as the switchers' export activity is lower than the non-switchers' export activity. In the author's view, this can be explained by the fact that family firms are concerned with family wealth, and when this is threatened they are more likely to take riskier decisions related to internationalization than the family firms switching to non-family control. Exporting is more hazardous than selling domestically, but if selling only domestically threatens the firms' survival and the family wealth, family firms are more eager to export to protect their family wealth (Cesinger et al., 2016; Liu et al., 2011).

Within the stream of studies on governance and export in family firms, Majocchi et al. (2018) emphasized the beneficial effect of having outside owners and managers, both independently and jointly, for export activities in family SMEs. In their view, the presence of outside owners and managers represent a signal that the family firm has opened up its governance structure and successfully overcome the so-called "*bifurcation bias*" which lead the family firm towards inefficient decision-making and therefore may result in reduced internationalization.

In investigating the relationships between the presence of a family leader and internationalization, Bauweraerts et al. (2019) confirmed the idea that family management can be harmful for export intensity in family SMEs. However, their study interestingly showed that the role of the Board of Directors is especially important, as it is able "*to turn the tide*" so that the family CEO effect becomes positive. Specifically, their focus is on the board's service role which typically consists in equipping the CEO with information, counselling, resources, and crucial social relationships, with positive implications on decision-making processes and the execution of successful strategies. With respect to the Board of Directors and its impact on export activities, another key aspect under the scholarly attention is the presence of family involvement. Nevertheless, empirical evidence is still mixed. Some studies found that family involvement in the Board of Directors increases international sales because of the stewardship effect of family members that wish to maintain the business in the long run for the benefit of current and future generations (Zahra, 2003); other scholars suggested that family involvement in the Board of Directors hampers the strategic independence of the management team and reduces the access to critical resources for export (Calabrò et al., 2009); still others demonstrated that the relationship between family involvement in the Board of Directors and international sales is non-linear and to understand this complex relationship an integration among stewardship, stagnation, and upper echelons perspectives is needed (Sciascia et al., 2013).

Beyond corporate governance considerations, also other distinctive aspects of the family business influence international sales. For example, Merino et al. (2015) provided evidence on a sample of 500 Spanish firms that the family experience—gained through the succession processes among different generations—and its culture orientation—in terms of overlapping between the family and the business, including the family's commitment to the business—positively affect the firm's export activity, whilst the degree of overall dominance in the hands of family members via ownership, management, and governance does not have any significant influence.

Broadly speaking, it is possible to observe that previous studies either implicitly or explicitly assumed that family involvement in the business at various levels of the firm's governance generate distinctive features which strongly drive the firm's behavior towards export, with mixed findings. Pongelli et al. (2021b) noted that previous studies all built on the theoretical assumption that different types of owners hold different goals but have overlooked to investigate directly the impact of these goals on export. To this end, the study by Pongelli et al. (2021b) showed that the pursuit of different types of family-centered goals may lead family firms to pursue the facilitative *versus* restrictive approach. The authors considered export as a mixed gamble according to which family firms can get favorable outcomes, such as the access to new markets and new resources, but as mentioned previously, may also incur potential losses, (such as increased costs and related international risks), as well as specific threats to the family's socioemotional wealth. The perception of this mixed gamble may vary across family firms depending on the effective emphasis that the family owners place on family-centered goals considered as a multidimensional construct that encompasses both non-economic (e.g., family harmony and family reputation) and economic (e.g., family financial security and the achievement of a desirable lifestyle) aspects. According to this study, the different emphasis placed on family-centered non-economic and family-centered economic goals may influence the family owners' risk preferences related to internationalization, promoting either a *restrictive* (risk averse) or *facilitating* (risk seeking) approach towards internationalization, with negative and/or positive implications for export performance.

Non-equity Contractual Agreements

Beyond export, other non-equity entry modes usually takes the form of contractual agreements (also called non-equity strategic alliances) (Pan & Tse, 2000). Unfortunately, to the best of our knowledge, the scholarly attention over non-equity contractual agreements as foreign market entry modes for family firms is still very limited. Although not providing specific insights on this type of entry mode, some qualitative studies on family firms' internationalization mention the adoption of contractual agreements by family firms. For instance, the explorative article by Okoroafo (1999) provided evidence that both joint ventures and non-equity contractual agreements are the second most-used entry mode after export. Later on, Claver et al. (2009) investigated family-related factors which lead family firms to engage in entry mode with a gradual increase in the degree of commitment namely, exports, contractual agreements, joint ventures, and wholly owned subsidiaries. More precisely, they find empirical support that long-term vision, the presence of non-family managers and the low importance attached to self-financing are associated with entry modes with higher international commitment. Besides, Andreu et al. (2020) relying on a sample of 981 hotels established abroad by 76 Spanish hotel chains, showed also that family involvement is associated with entry modes involving greater control and resource commitment.

Within the wide array of contractual agreements, franchising is one of the most commonly used. It represents a type of non-equity cooperation and occurs when the owner of a business system (labeled as franchisor) sells to an individual or a firm (namely the franchisee) the right to market its branded products (goods or services) and uses its business practices (Combs et al., 2004). Despite its wide diffusion in the practice both at national and international level, only a few studies investigated this type of contractual agreement in the family business context. With the exception of Kaufmann (1999) and Udell (1973) which are the only two studies on franchising and family business issues before the last ten years, the article by Chirico et al. (2011) represents the first effort to develop a conceptual study on this topic. Specifically, their theoretical work argued that *familiness*, resulting from the enduring interaction of the family and the business (Habbershon & Williams, 1999) provides a distinctive bundle of intangible resources that may be especially fruitful to franchising activities. Subsequently, Patel et al. (2018) empirically investigated the influence of family ownership on franchisee financial performance and found that family-owned franchisees achieve lower sales per employee than non-family-owned franchisees. More recently, Chirico and colleagues integrated this result and provided both theoretical and empirical evidence that family firm franchisors behave and perform differently compared to non-family firm franchisors. While family firm franchisors generally cultivates stronger relationships with their franchisees and provides them with more training, they generate lower performance compared to the non-family firm franchisors. Interestingly, they also showed that the negative effect on performance becomes positive when family firm franchisors are older and larger (Chirico et al., 2021).

2.3 Family Firms and Equity-Based Entry Modes

A growing body of studies within the stream of research on family firms and entry modes is devoting scholarly attention to equity-based entry modes. While only a few of these contributions address this topic from a decisional perspective (i.e. the strategic decision between entering a foreign market through either an equity investment or export) (Carney et al., 2017; Scholes et al., 2016; Shanmugasundaram, 2019) all of them have a common focus on foreign direct investments. This is visible also from the specific terminology they use, introducing labels such as "*multinationality*" to emphasize the advanced form of internationalization under investigation (e.g., Cesinger et al., 2016; Mondal et al., 2022). This *corpus* of studies provided several interesting insights into the family business field, summarized into five main points.

Firstly, family firms are found to be particularly advantaged with respect to exporting, but less well-suited for the high levels of coordination required for extensive outward foreign direct investments (Carney et al., 2017). A qualitative research developed by Scholes et al. (2016) confirms this finding. Relying on interviews with six family firms in Singapore, their study indicated that initial internationalization through exports is enabled due to family networks, but as mentioned previously, the distinctive family-related desire to maintain family harmony and aversion towards outsiders may negatively influence network creation and resource development, which then constrains the extent to which the firm internationalizes beyond exporting. In the same vein, based on longitudinal data on 2152 publicly listed Indian firms, Singh and Delios (2017) showed that family ownership is negatively related to the number of new domestic ventures initiated by a firm. Conversely, Arregle et al. (2017) found no differences between family firms and non-family firms in their number of foreign subsidiaries (i.e. international scale). However, their results also showed that family firms internationalize less than other firms in terms of geographic scope. Going deeper into this direction and addressing the sources of heterogeneous behavior in family firms, Shanmugasundaram (2019) demonstrated that if the ownership concentration of family firms is not high, they go international through foreign direct investments; if the ownership concentration increases, the internationalization of the firms it restricts exports. Jimenez et al. (2019) argued that it is not family ownership itself that matters but rather ownership and the presence on the Board of Directors to drive family firms towards a lower scope of their foreign direct investments compared to non-family firms. Indeed, their results emphasize that family firms show a different pattern of behavior but only when the family simultaneously has majority ownership and board presence. Similarly, Ray et al. (2018) and Mondal et al. (2022) demonstrated also that the presence of family members at the managerial level is negatively related to the scale and scope of the family firm's multinationality, thereby suggesting that family-managed firms are more averse to internationalization than family firms managed by non-family professionals. As a mirror finding, sophisticated financial management and external ownership are deemed to foster foreign direct investments in family firms (Dick et al., 2017).

Secondly, a recent study by Fourné and Zschoche (2020) based on a large sample of German family firms introduced a different perspective and suggests that family firms pursue trait-based imitation to reduce uncertainty in follow-up foreign direct investments. More precisely, the authors showed that family firms imitate successful peers that are also owned by a family, especially during the initial years in a foreign market, when the firm is publicly listed or as performance falls below social aspiration. Likewise, also Mondal et al. (2021) conceptualized foreign direct investments in family firms as a reactive behavior. Specifically, their results suggest that family firms increase their existing *outward* foreign direct investments in response to *inward* foreign direct investments announcements by foreign multinational companies. Results also demonstrated that the outward FDI-growth response varies across family firms and is influenced by heterogeneity in the management type (professional/family-based), the level of foreign institutional ownership, and whether the family CEO's possess international experience (or not). Another recent study brings new insights to the understanding of family firms' foreign direct investments by shedding light on the divestment decisions related to foreign subsidiaries (Kim et al., 2019). By providing evidence on a sample of 161 Korean manufacturing family MNEs between 1998 and 2003, this study demonstrated that family firms with a family CEO are less likely to divest than non-family CEOs. They also showed that family CEOs avoid divesting foreign subsidiaries with larger affective endowments, particularly those under family control through threshold ownership and those located in host countries where families have already lost ownership of subsidiaries through past divestitures.

Thirdly, beyond either the scale or scope of foreign direct investment, other studies within this group address equity-based internationalization with a different focus i.e. sourcing decisions and location choices. Specifically, with respect to sourcing decisions, Horgos (2013) introduced the idea that international sourcing was differently managed between family and non-family firms. More recently, Pongelli et al. (2019) demonstrated using a sample of 1180 European firms that family firms are more likely than non-family firms to engage in captive offshoring (i.e. foreign direct investments for sourcing purposes) rather than offshore outsourcing (i.e. buying from foreign suppliers). Interestingly, they also found that family firms are more successful than non-family firms when they revise their preferences and undertake offshore outsourcing. With respect to location choices instead, we find three interesting studies revealing that: family firms are less likely to invest in developed markets and more likely to invest in developing countries than non-family firms (Bhaumik & Driffield, 2011); having family management in subsidiaries increases the likelihood of engagement in host regions (Chung, 2014); higher family involvement corresponds to a lower number of foreign direct investments in psychically distant countries (Baronchelli et al., 2016).

Fourthly, several studies within this group introduced equity-based internationalization exclusively from the empirical side i.e. through the way they measured internationalization. Since the focus on equity based internationalization comes only in the method section, this body of literature does not offer a theoretical contribution to the understanding of family firms' internationalization beyond export but has the merit of providing a measure of internationalization that includes the international endeavors of family firms which embark into foreign direct investments. For example, in their study on the effect of government political ideology on internationalization of family-controlled firms, Duran et al. (2017) measured internationalization as a composite index including both foreign sales and foreign direct investments. With a similar measure of internationalization based on both export and foreign direct investments, Liang et al. (2014) showed that family involvement in management has an inverted-U-shaped relationship with the likelihood of internationalization and that the percentage of family ownership has a U-shaped relationship with the likelihood of internationalization. Consistent measures to proxy internationalization are also provided by Lin and Wang (2021), Liu et al. (2011), Purkayastha et al. (2018) and Manogna and Mishra (2021). Instead, other studies provided measures of internationalization based on foreign direct investments exclusively. This is the case, for example, of Zahra (2020) that showed that family-controlled firms had significantly lower scale and scope in the Asia pacific region compared to non-family firms. To operationalize the international scope, the author considered the number of foreign subsidiaries differently from older studies which relied purely on the number of countries in which the family firm was selling its products in order to measure the same construct (Zahra, 2003). Furthermore, Singla et al. (2017) measured internationalization through the assets of foreign affiliates and found that while family owners with lower levels of ownership favor their firms' internationalization, they do not favor it at higher levels of ownership.

Finally, a number of studies on equity-based internationalization focuses on emerging markets, especially China and India. While some contributions in this stream of literature investigate these contexts as "host" or target countries (e.g., Lien & Filatotchev, 2015), most of them addresses emerging markets as "home" or domestic countries. In the Chinese context, Wei et al. (2020) investigated how different family firm types affect the decisions on foreign direct investments. They showed that Chinese family firms owned by a lone founder have higher propensity and intensity of foreign direct investments than those owned by multiple family members. Jin et al. (2021) provided empirical evidence on a sample of 2704 small family businesses in China that family reputation has a positive effect on equity-based internationalization, whilst family involvement has a negative effect. In the same geographic context, Tsang (2002, 2020) examined the foreign direct investments behavior of Chinese family businesses from an organizational learning perspective and suggested that family firms compared to non-family firms generally use an informal and unstructured approach to foreign direct investments, often sending family members overseas to be in charge of key management positions. This has negative implications for organizational learning because owing to the highly centralized management control and strategic decision making, strategic experience gained from an foreign direct investment process is largely held within the family, particularly the head of family. Similarly two studies developed in the context of Taiwanese family business groups investigated the strategic usage of family managers in foreign subsidiaries (Chung et al., 2021; Chung & Dahms, 2019). Their contention is that family managers represent a specific resource used to mitigate institutional uncertainty caused by larger institutional distances occurring between the home and host countries. Also India is attracting the attention of scholars, starting from the study by Bhaumik et al. (2010) which demonstrated using a sample of Indian pharmaceutical firms that family firms are less likely to invest overseas ventures than non-family firms (for more recent studies in the Indian context see, Mondal et al., 2022; Singh & Delios, 2017; Shanmugasundaram, 2019; Singla et al., 2017).

Joint Ventures and Wholly Owned Subsidiaries

Previous studies on joint ventures and wholly-owned subsidiaries are summarized together as almost half of the scholarly contributions about these entry modes in the family business field addresses the choice between them rather than focusing on only one of them. This decision, known in the international business literature as the subsidiary ownership choice, refers to the choice about the ownership structure of foreign subsidiaries. Either parent companies have equal ownership or one of them holds a greater ownership share, a joint venture is a firm that is set up, owned and operated by two or more companies. Instead, a wholly-owned subsidiary is a firm totally owned by a single firm which therefore holds total control over it (Erramilli, 1996; Makino & Neupert, 2000).

The attention of family business scholars over the subsidiary ownership choice begins during the 90s' when Swinth and Vinton (1993) argued that joint ventures are more successful when both parent companies are family firms. In their view, being a family firm means having values and goals in common which allow to bridge cultural barriers with external actors more effectively than publicly held corporations. Debellis and colleagues also proposed that the higher leadership unity and resource fluidity which family firms have lead to a greater ability to govern the complexities of the relationship between the parent companies, thus softening opportunistic hazards, and significantly increasing the likelihood of the long-term success of the international joint venture (Debellis et al., 2020). Pant and Rajadhyaksha (1996) also highlighted that evidence of family stability, structured succession plans and professional decision-making represent attractive characteristics for foreign actors who are interested in partnering with a family firm under a joint venture agreement. These intuitions have then been corroborated by a recent study which provided evidence on a dataset of 951 foreign investments that if both the investing and the local firm are family firms, forming a joint venture is preferred, while if only the investing firm is a family firm, a wholly-owned subsidiary is more likely (Sestu & Majocchi, 2020).

Yet, family firms seems to prefer more to remain independent compared with non-family businesses and therefore tend to engage less into joint ventures (Abdellatif et al., 2010; Debellis et al., 2020), especially when the family firm has a family leader (Pongelli et al., 2021a). Despite that, the reluctance to embark on a joint venture can be mitigated under certain vulnerability conditions which push the family decision makers to make decisions out of their comfort zone (Pongelli et al., 2021b). Specifically, when lacking international experience (Kuo et al., 2012) entering into a highly unfamiliar and distant countries (Del Bosco & Bettinelli, 2020; Loehde et al., 2020) or facing high internal and environmental uncertainty (Kao et al., 2013; Kao & Kuo, 2017) even family firms with high levels of family involvement are willing to adjust their strategic preference toward wholly-owned subsidiaries and welcome joint ventures.

International Acquisitions and Greenfield Investments

As a final group of studies and consistent with the previous section, family firms' international acquisitions and greenfield investments are discussed jointly as they usually fall under the common category of studies on the foreign direct investments' establishment mode. This means that when an investing firm establishes a foreign subsidiary it must decide between forming a new venture through a greenfield investment or alternatively, acquiring an existing firm (Brouthers & Brouthers, 2000). However, the majority of previous studies were aimed to understand differences between family and non-family firms and are focused on acquisitions only rather than the establishment mode choice.

Previous studies highlighted that the attitude of family firms towards acquisitions is still controversial. While some studies suggested that international acquisitions are more attractive to family firms due to the benefits of risk diversification and loose-coupling (Haider et al., 2021); others found that a U-shaped relationship between family blockholding of voting rights and the relative size of international acquisitions (Chen et al., 2021) but others indicates that the family firms are less likely to make a cross-border acquisition than their non-family counterparts (Ossorio, 2019) especially during "*waves*" of cross-border acquisitions characterized by higher risk and uncertainty (Fuad et al., 2021a, 2021b). Moreover, different forms of ownership structures (Geppert et al., 2013) and ownership similarities between the acquiring and the acquired firms (Bettinazzi et al., 2020) also influences the likelihood for an acquisition. Interestingly, Worek et al. (2018) showed that the distinctive characteristics of family firms influence the goals that they want to achieve if they put in place an acquisition. Specifically, family firms are deemed to have more goals related to stakeholders and market competitiveness than non-family firms, and fewer financial and innovation goals.

With respect to the choice between the two establishment modes, with the exception of a recent study by Rienda et al. (2019) suggesting that family firms prefer acquisitions instead of greenfield investments, previous research seems to point towards the conclusion that family firms are more likely to settle in greenfield investment and full equity ownership in order to maintain family owners' socioemotional wealth (Yamanoi & Asaba, 2018). This conclusion is based on the notion that family owners can design and manage foreign subsidiaries at their own discretion in the case of a greenfield investment, whilst they are forced to collaborate with local managers to modify an existing local firm in the case of an international acquisition.

In the same vein, the article by Boellis et al. (2016) represents an interesting effort to investigate family firms heterogeneity and show that family involvement both in the firm ownership and management leads to a higher propensity towards greenfield initiatives (*versus* acquisitions). However, they also found that such a propensity decreases with international experience especially in family-owned firms given the greater ability of professionalized management to overcome family-related concerns on making acquisitions. A more recent study (Mariotti et al., 2021) corroborates these results demonstrating that controlling families prefer greenfield investments when their attachment to the firm is high. Moreover, according to the authors the entry strategy depends on a socio-emotionally-driven selection process triggered by succession as family firms run by second generations show a stronger orientation towards acquisitions.

2.4 Concluding Remarks

The description of this extensive but fragmented area of research unveiled specific features on family firms' different types of entry modes into international markets and also revealed some common paths which make it possible to draw a main concluding consideration. Overall, although high levels of family ownership seem to make family firms less confident to embark on high commitment entry modes, it is plausible to infer that family ownership alone has a low predicting power to understand entry modes decisions into the family business domain, especially when used to compare family and non-family firms. Indeed, entry modes decisions must be conceptualized as influenced by a variety of factors, both internal and external to the family firm. At the firm level, beside the family ownership level and composition, also other types of family involvement in the business attracted the scholarly attention for their influence over entry modes, such as, among the others family leadership and family presence in the Board of Directors, as well as the specific individual-level characteristics of family members in charge of international operations. Indeed, the type and the extent of family involvement lead to different risk preferences with implications on the international entry mode choices. Moreover, family firms' entry modes choices are also determined by contextual factors like the home and the host context of different institutions and the cultural aspects which could influence the degree of perceived uncertainty over the foreign investment.

References

Abdellatif, M., Amann, B., & Jaussaud, J. (2010). Family versus non-family business: A comparison of international strategies. *Journal of Family Business Strategy, 1*(2), 108–116. https://doi.org/10.1016/j.jfbs.2010.04.004

Anderson, E., & Gatignon, H. (1986). Modes of foreign entry: A transaction cost analysis and propositions. *Journal of International Business Studies, 17*(3), 1–26. https://doi.org/10.1057/palgrave.jibs.8490432

Andreu, R., Claver-Cortés, E., Quer, D., & Rienda, L. (2020). Family involvement and Spanish hotel chains' entry modes abroad. *Current Issues in Tourism, 23*(11), 1375–1393. https://doi.org/10.1080/13683500.2019.1620186

Arregle, J.-L., Duran, P., Hitt, M. A., & van Essen, M. (2017). Why is family firms' internationalization unique? A meta-analysis. *Entrepreneurship Theory and Practice, 41*(5), 801–831. https://doi.org/10.1111/etap.12246

Baronchelli, G., Bettinelli, C., Del Bosco, B., & Loane, S. (2016). The impact of family involvement on the investments of Italian small-medium enterprises in psychically distant countries. *International Business Review, 25*(4), 960–970. https://doi.org/10.1016/j.ibusrev.2016.01.011

Bauweraerts, J., Sciascia, S., Naldi, L., & Mazzola, P. (2019). Family CEO and board service: Turning the tide for export scope in family SMEs. *International Business Review, 28*(5), 101583. https://doi.org/10.1016/j.ibusrev.2019.05.003

Bettinazzi, E. L., Miller, D., Amore, M. D., & Corbetta, G. (2020). Ownership similarity in mergers and acquisitions target selection. *Strategic Organization, 18*(2), 330–361. https://doi.org/10.1177/1476127018801294

Bhaumik, S. K., & Driffield, N. (2011). Direction of outward FDI of EMNEs: Evidence from the Indian pharmaceutical sector. *Thunderbird International Business Review, 53*(5), 615–628. https://doi.org/10.1002/tie.20438

Bhaumik, S. K., Driffield, N., & Pal, S. (2010). Does ownership structure of emerging-market firms affect their outward FDI? The case of the Indian automotive and pharmaceutical sectors. *Journal of International Business Studies, 41*(3), 437–450. https://doi.org/10.1057/jibs.2009.52

Boellis, A., Mariotti, S., Minichilli, A., & Piscitello, L. (2016). Family involvement and firms' establishment mode choice in foreign markets. *Journal of International Business Studies, 47*(8), 929–950. https://doi.org/10.1057/jibs.2016.23

Brouthers, K. D., & Brouthers, L. E. (2000). Acquisition or greenfield start-up? Institutional, cultural and transaction cost influences. *Strategic Management Journal, 21*(1), 89–97. https://doi.org/10.1002/(SICI)1097-0266(200001)21:1<89::AID-SMJ85>3.0.CO;2-8

Brouthers, K. D., & Hennart, J. F. (2007). Boundaries of the firm: Insights from international entry mode research. *Journal of Management, 33*(3), 395–425. https://doi.org/10.1177/0149206307300817

Calabrò, A., Mussolino, D., & Huse, M. (2009). The role of board of directors in the internationalisation process of small and medium sized family businesses. *International Journal of Globalisation and Small Business, 3*(4), 393–411.

Calabrò, A., Brogi, M., & Torchia, M. (2016). What does really matter in the internationalization of small and medium-sized family businesses? *Journal of Small Business Management, 54*(2), 679–696. https://doi.org/10.1111/jsbm.12165

Cano-Rubio, M., Lombardi, R., Fuentes-Lombardo, G., & Núñez-Cacho, P. (2021). Familiness, business strategy and stakeholder engagement: The internationalisation of Spanish olive oil mills. *Business Strategy and the Environment, 30*(8), 4258–4280. https://doi.org/10.1002/bse.2868

Carney, M., Duran, P., van Essen, M., & Shapiro, D. (2017). Family firms, internationalization, and national competitiveness: Does family firm prevalence matter? *Journal of Family Business Strategy, 8*(3), 123–136. https://doi.org/10.1016/j.jfbs.2017.06.001

Cesinger, B., Hughes, M., Mensching, H., Bouncken, R., Fredrich, V., & Kraus, S. (2016). A socioemotional wealth perspective on how collaboration intensity, trust, and international market knowledge affect family firms' multinationality. *Journal of World Business, 51*(4), 586–599. https://doi.org/10.1016/j.jwb.2016.02.004

Chen, J., Sousa, C. M., & Xinming, H. (2016). The determinants of export performance: A review of the literature 2006–2014. *International Marketing Review, 33*(5), 626–670. https://doi.org/10.1108/imr-10-2015-0212

Chen, V. Z., Hobdari, B., Kellermanns, F. W., & Sluhan, A. (2021). For love or money? Family versus financial blockholders in international acquisitions. *Corporate Governance: An International Review, 30*(2), 140–160. https://doi.org/10.1111/corg.12392

Chirico, F., Ireland, R. D., & Sirmon, D. G. (2011). Franchising and the family firm: Creating unique sources of advantage through "familiness". *Entrepreneurship Theory and Practice, 35*(3), 483–501. https://doi.org/10.1111/j.1540-6520.2011.00441.x

Chirico, F., Welsh, D. H., Ireland, R. D., & Sieger, P. (2021). Family versus non-family firm franchisors: Behavioural and performance differences. *Journal of Management Studies, 58*(1), 165–200. https://doi.org/10.1111/joms.12567

Cho, J., & Lee, J. W. (2017). The impact of ownership structure on internationalization: An empirical study of Korean SMEs. *Global Business & Finance Review (GBFR), 22*(1), 51–66. https://doi.org/10.17549/gbfr.2017.22.1.51

Chung, H.-M. (2014). The role of family management and ownership on semi-globalization pattern of globalization: The case of family business groups.

International Business Review, 23(1), 260–271. https://doi.org/10.1016/j.ibusrev.2013.04.005

Chung, H.-M., & Dahms, S. (2019). Leadership decisions in foreign subsidiaries of multinational family business groups. *The International Journal of Human Resource Management*, 4629–4658. https://doi.org/10.1080/09585192.2019.1660699

Chung, H.-M., Dahms, S., & Kao, P. T. (2021). Emerging market multinational family business groups and the use of family managers in foreign subsidiaries. *Management International Review, 61*(1), 57–89. https://doi.org/10.1007/s11575-021-00437-y

Claver, E., Rienda, L., & Quer, D. (2009). Family firms' international commitment: The influence of family-related factors. *Family Business Review, 22*(2), 125–135. https://doi.org/10.1177/0894486508330054

Colli, A., García-Canal, E., & Guillén, M. F. (2013). Family character and international entrepreneurship: A historical comparison of Italian and Spanish 'new multinationals'. *Business History, 55*(1), 119–138. https://doi.org/10.1080/00076791.2012.687536

Combs, J. G., Michael, S., & Castrogiovanni, G. (2004). Franchising: A review and avenues to greater theoretical diversity. *Journal of Management, 30*, 907–931. https://doi.org/10.1016/j.jm.2004.06.006

Debellis, F., De Massis, A., Messeni Petruzzelli, A., Frattini, F., & Del Giudice, M. (2020). Strategic agility and international joint ventures: The willingness-ability paradox of family firms. *Journal of International Management, 27*(1), 100739. https://doi.org/10.1016/j.intman.2020.100739

Del Bosco, B., & Bettinelli, C. (2020). How do family SMEs control their investments abroad? The role of distance and family control. *Management International Review, 60*(1), 1–35. https://doi.org/10.1007/s11575-019-00406-6

Dick, M., Mitter, C., Feldbauer-Durstmüller, B. F., & Pernsteiner, H. (2017). The impact of finance and governance on the internationalisation modes of family firms. *European Journal of International Management, 11*(1), 42–64. https://doi.org/10.1504/EJIM.2017.081254

Duran, P., Kostova, T., & van Essen, M. (2017). Political ideologies and the internationalization of family-controlled firms. *Journal of World Business, 52*(4), 474–488. https://doi.org/10.1016/j.jwb.2016.07.001

Erramilli, M. K. (1996). Nationality and subsidiary ownership patterns in multinational corporations. *Journal of International Business Studies, 27*(2), 225–248. https://doi.org/10.1057/palgrave.jibs.8490133

Fernandez, Z., & Nieto, M. J. (2005). Internationalization strategy of small and medium-sized family businesses: Some influential factors. *Family Business Review, 8*(1), 77–89. https://doi.org/10.1111/j.1741-6248.2005.00031.x

Fernandez, Z., & Nieto, M. J. (2006). Impact of ownership on the international involvement of SMEs. *Journal of International Business Studies, 37*, 340–351. https://doi.org/10.1057/palgrave.jibs.8400196

Fourné, S. P. L., & Zschoche, M. (2020). Reducing uncertainty in follow-up foreign direct investment: Imitation by family firms. *Global Strategy Journal, 10*(4), 839–860. https://doi.org/10.1002/gsj.1331

Fuad, M., Thakur, V., & Sinha, A. K. (2021a). Entry timing as a mixed gamble in cross-border acquisition waves: A study of family firms. *Family Business Review, 34*(3), 323–341. https://doi.org/10.1177/08944865211026175

Fuad, M., Thakur, V., & Sinha, A. K. (2021b). Family firms and their participation in cross-border acquisition waves: Evidence from India. *Cross Cultural & Strategic Management, 28*(4), 791–814. https://doi.org/10.1108/CCSM-05-2020-0107

Geppert, M., Dörrenbächer, C., Gammelgaard, J., & Taplin, I. (2013). Managerial risk-taking in international acquisitions in the brewery industry: Institutional and ownership influences compared. *British Journal of Management, 24*(3), 316–332. https://doi.org/10.1111/j.1467-8551.2011.00806.x

Habbershon, T. G., & Williams, M. L. (1999). A resource-based framework for assessing the strategic advantages of family firms. *Family Business Review, 12*, 1–25. https://doi.org/10.1111/j.1741-6248.1999.00001.x

Haider, Z. A., Li, J., Wang, Y., & Wu, Z. (2021). Do family firms have higher or lower deal valuations? A contextual analysis. *Entrepreneurship Theory and Practice, 45*(4), 709–739. https://doi.org/10.1177/1042258720910950

Hennart, J. F., & Slangen, A. H. (2014). Yes, we really do need more entry mode studies! A commentary on Shaver. *Journal of International Business Studies, 46*(1), 114–122. https://doi.org/10.1057/jibs.2014.39

Horgos, D. (2013). Global sourcing: A family-firm's perspective. *Journal of Small Business & Entrepreneurship, 26*(3), 221–240. https://doi.org/10.1080/08276331.2013.808028

Jimenez, A., Majocchi, A., & Della Piana, B. (2019). Not all family firms are equal: The moderating effect of family involvement on the political risk exposure of the foreign direct investment portfolio. Preliminary evidence from Spanish multinational enterprises. *Thunderbird International Business Review, 61*(2), 309–323. https://doi.org/10.1002/tie.22032

Jin, C., Wu, B., & Hu, Y. (2021). Family business internationalization in paradox: Effects of socioemotional wealth and entrepreneurial spirit. *Frontiers in Psychology, 12*, 667615. https://doi.org/10.3389/fpsyg.2021.667615

Kao, M.-S., & Kuo, A. (2017). The effect of uncertainty on FDI entry mode decisions: The influence of family ownership and involvement in the board of directors. *Journal of Family Business Strategy, 8*(4), 224–236. https://doi.org/10.1016/j.jfbs.2017.09.003

Kao, M.-S., Kuo, A., & Chang, Y.-C. (2013). How family control influences FDI entry mode choice. *Journal of Management & Organization, 19*(4), 367–385. https://doi.org/10.1017/jmo.2013.23

Kaufmann, P. J. (1999). Franchising and the choice of self-employment. *Journal of Business Venturing, 14*(4), 345–362. https://doi.org/10.1016/S0883-9026(98)00021-4

Kim, H., Hoskisson, R. E., & Zyung, J. D. (2019). Socioemotional favoritism: Evidence from foreign divestitures in family multinationals. *Organization Studies, 40*(6), 917–940. https://doi.org/10.1177/0170840619838955

Kontinen, T., & Ojala, A. (2012). Internationalization pathways among family-owned SMEs. *International Marketing Review, 29*(5), 496–518. https://doi.org/10.1108/02651331211260359

Kuo, A., Kao, M. S., Chang, Y. C., & Chiu, C. F. (2012). The influence of international experience on entry mode choice: Difference between family and non-family firms. *European Management Journal, 30*(3), 248–263. https://doi.org/10.1016/j.emj.2012.03.008

Liang, X., Wang, L., & Cui, Z. (2014). Chinese private firms and internationalization. *Family Business Review, 27*(2), 126–141. https://doi.org/10.1177/0894486513480885

Lien, Y.-C., & Filatotchev, I. (2015). Ownership characteristics as determinants of FDI location decisions in emerging economies. *Journal of World Business, 50*(4), 637–650. https://doi.org/10.1016/j.jwb.2014.09.002

Lin, W.-T., & Wang, L. C. (2021). Family firms, R&D, and internationalization: The stewardship and socio-emotional wealth perspectives. *Asia Pacific Journal of Management, 38*(1), 91–119. https://doi.org/10.1007/s10490-018-9636-2

Liu, Y., Lin, W.-T., & Cheng, K.-Y. (2011). Family ownership and the international involvement of Taiwan's high-technology firms: The moderating effect of high-discretion organizational slack. *Management and Organization Review, 7*(2), 201–222. https://doi.org/10.1111/j.1740-8784.2011.00220.x

Loehde, A. S. K., Calabrò, A., Torchia, M., & Kraus, S. (2020). Joint (ad)ventures – Family firms' international entry mode choices for emerging markets. *International Journal of Entrepreneurial Behavior & Research, 26*(6), 1235–1258. https://doi.org/10.1108/IJEBR-10-2019-0573

Majocchi, A., D'Angelo, A., Forlani, E., & Buck, T. (2018). Bifurcation bias and exporting: Can foreign work experience be an answer? Insight from European family SMEs. *Journal of World Business, 53*(2), 237–247. https://doi.org/10.1016/j.jwb.2017.11.005

Makino, S., & Neupert, K. E. (2000). National culture, transaction costs, and the choice between joint venture and wholly owned subsidiary. *Journal of International Business Studies, 31*(4), 705–713. https://doi.org/10.1057/palgrave.jibs.8490930

Manogna, R. L., & Mishra, A. K. (2021). Exploring the role of family ownership in internationalization: Empirical investigation of Indian firms. *Review of International Business and Strategy, 31*(1), 1–15. https://doi.org/10.1108/RIBS-05-2020-0058

Mariotti, S., Marzano, R., & Piscitello, L. (2021). The role of family firms' generational heterogeneity in the entry mode choice in foreign markets. *Journal of Business Research, 132*, 800–812. https://doi.org/10.1016/j.jbusres.2020.10.064

Merino, F., Monreal-Pérez, J., & Sánchez-Marín, G. (2015). Family SMEs' internationalization: Disentangling the influence of familiness on Spanish firms' export activity. *Journal of Small Business Management, 53*(4), 1164–1184. https://doi.org/10.1111/jsbm.12111

Mondal, A., Lahiri, S., & Ray, S. (2021). Strategic response to inward foreign direct investment: A study of Indian family firms. *Management International Review, 61*(2), 207–233. https://doi.org/10.1007/s11575-021-00441-2

Mondal, A., Ray, S., & Lahiri, S. (2022). Family ownership, family management, and multinationality: Evidence from India. *Journal of Business Research, 138*, 347–359. https://doi.org/10.1016/j.jbusres.2021.09.017

Monreal-Pérez, J., & Sánchez-Marín, G. (2017). Does transitioning from family to non-family controlled firm influence internationalization? *Journal of Small Business and Enterprise Development, 24*(4), 775–792. https://doi.org/10.1108/JSBED-02-2017-0029

Okoroafo, S. C. (1999). Internationalization of family businesses: Evidence from Northwest Ohio, U.S.A. *Family Business Review, 12*(2), 147–158. https://doi.org/10.1111/j.1741-6248.1999.00147.x

Ossorio, M. (2019). Cross-border acquisitions and family businesses. *EuroMed Journal of Business, 14*(2), 78–91. https://doi.org/10.1108/EMJB-05-2018-0033

Pan, Y., & Tse, D. K. (2000). The hierarchical model of market entry modes. *Journal of International Business Studies, 31*(4), 535–554. https://doi.org/10.1057/palgrave.jibs.8490921

Pant, P. N., & Rajadhyaksha, V. G. (1996). Partnership with an Asian family business – What every multinational corporation should know. *Long Range Planning, 29*(6), 812–820. https://doi.org/10.1016/S0024-6301(97)82818-X

Pascucci, F., Domenichelli, O., Peruffo, E., & Gregori, G. L. (2021). Family ownership and the export performance of SMEs: The moderating role of financial constraints and flexibility. *Journal of Small Business and Enterprise Development.* (ahead of print). https://doi.org/10.1108/JSBED-03-2021-0113

Patel, P. C., Kim, K. Y., Devaraj, S., & Li, M. (2018). Family ties that b(l)ind: Do family-owned franchisees have lower financial performance than non-family-owned franchisees? *Journal of Retailing, 94*(2), 231–245. https://doi.org/10.1016/j.jretai.2017.12.001

Pongelli, C., Caroli, M. G., & Cucculelli, M. (2016). Family business going abroad: The effect of family ownership on foreign market entry mode decisions. *Small Business Economics, 47*(3), 787–801. https://doi.org/10.1007/s11187-016-9763-4

Pongelli, C., Calabrò, A., & Basco, R. (2019). Family firms' international make-or-buy decisions: Captive offshoring, offshore outsourcing, and the role of home region focus. *Journal of Business Research, 103*, 596–606. https://doi.org/10.1016/j.jbusres.2018.02.033

Pongelli, C., Calabrò, A., Quarato, F., Minichilli, A., & Corbetta, G. (2021a). Out of the comfort zone! Family leaders' subsidiary ownership choices and the role of vulnerabilities. *Family Business Review, 34*(4), 404–424. https://doi.org/10.1177/08944865211050858

Pongelli, C., Valentino, A., Calabrò, A., & Caroli, M. G. (2021b). Family-centered goals, geographic focus and family firms' internationalization: A study on export performance. *Entrepreneurship & Regional Development, 33*(7–8), 580–598. https://doi.org/10.1080/08985626.2021.1925851

Purkayastha, S., Manolova, T. S., & Edelman, L. F. (2018). Business group effects on the R&D intensity-internationalization relationship: Empirical evidence from India. *Journal of World Business, 53*(2), 104–117. https://doi.org/10.1016/j.jwb.2016.11.004

Ray, S., Mondal, A., & Ramachandran, K. (2018). How does family involvement affect a firm's internationalization? An investigation of Indian family firms. *Global Strategy Journal, 8*(1), 73–105. https://doi.org/10.1002/gsj.1196

Rienda, L., Claver, E., Quer, D., & Andreu, R. (2019). Family businesses from emerging markets and choice of entry mode abroad: Insights from Indian firms. *Asian Business & Management, 18*(1), 6–30. https://doi.org/10.1057/s41291-018-00053-z

Scholes, L., Mustafa, M., & Chen, S. (2016). Internationalization of small family firms: The influence of family from a socioemotional wealth perspective. *Thunderbird International Business Review, 58*(2), 131–146. https://doi.org/10.1002/tie.21729

Sciascia, S., Mazzola, P., Astrachan, J. H., & Pieper, T. M. (2012). The role of family ownership in international entrepreneurship: Exploring nonlinear effects. *Small Business Economics, 38*(1), 15–31. https://doi.org/10.1007/s11187-010-9264-9

Sciascia, S., Mazzola, P., Astrachan, J. H., & Pieper, T. M. (2013). Family involvement in the board of directors: Effects on sales internationalization. *Journal of Small Business Management, 51*(1), 83–99. https://doi.org/10.1111/j.1540-627X.2012.00373.x

Sestu, M. C., & Majocchi, A. (2020). Family firms and the choice between wholly owned subsidiaries and joint ventures: A transaction costs perspective. *Entrepreneurship Theory and Practice, 44*(2), 211–232. https://doi.org/10.1177/1042258718797925

Shanmugasundaram, S. (2019). Internationalization and governance of Indian family-owned business groups. *Journal of Family Business Management, 10*(1), 76–94. https://doi.org/10.1108/JFBM-06-2019-0040

Singh, D., & Delios, A. (2017). Corporate governance, board networks and growth in domestic and international markets: Evidence from India. *Journal of World Business, 52*(5), 615–627. https://doi.org/10.1016/j.jwb.2017.02.002

Singla, C., George, R., & Veliyath, R. (2017). Ownership structure and internationalization of Indian firms. *Journal of Business Research, 81*, 130–143. https://doi.org/10.1016/j.jbusres.2017.08.016

Swinth, R. L., & Vinton, K. L. (1993). Do family-owned businesses have a strategic advantage in international joint ventures? *Family Business Review, 6*(1), 19–30. https://doi.org/10.1111/j.1741-6248.1993.00019.x

Tsang, E. W. (2002). Learning from overseas venturing experience. *Journal of Business Venturing, 17*(1), 21–40. https://doi.org/10.1016/S0883-9026(00)00052-5

Tsang, E. W. K. (2020). Family firms and internationalization: An organizational learning perspective. *Asia Pacific Journal of Management, 37*(1), 205–225. https://doi.org/10.1007/s10490-018-9590-z

Udell, G. (1973). Franchising: America's last small business frontier? *Journal of Small Business Management, 11*, 31–34.

Wei, Q., Luo, J., & Huang, X. (2020). Influence of social identity on family firms' FDI decisions: The moderating role of internal capital markets. *Management International Review, 60*(5), 651–693. https://doi.org/10.1007/s11575-020-00427-6

Worek, M., De Massis, A., Wright, M., & Veider, V. (2018). Acquisitions, disclosed goals and firm characteristics: A content analysis of family and non-family firms. *Journal of Family Business Strategy, 9*(4), 250–267. https://doi.org/10.1016/j.jfbs.2018.09.003

Xu, K., Hitt, M. A., & Miller, S. R. (2020). The ownership structure contingency in the sequential international entry mode decision process: Family owners and institutional investors in family-dominant versus family-influenced firms. *Journal of International Business Studies, 51*(2), 151–171. https://doi.org/10.1057/s41267-019-00250-8

Yamanoi, J., & Asaba, S. (2018). The impact of family ownership on establishment and ownership modes in foreign direct investment: The moderating role of corruption in host countries. *Global Strategy Journal, 8*(1), 106–135. https://doi.org/10.1002/gsj.1198

Yang, X., Li, J., Stanley, L. J., Kellermanns, F. W., & Li, X. (2020). How family firm characteristics affect internationalization of Chinese family SMEs. *Asia Pacific Journal of Management, 37*(2), 417–448. https://doi.org/10.1007/s10490-018-9579-7

Zahra, S. A. (2003). International expansion of US manufacturing family businesses: The effect of ownership and involvement. *Journal of Business Venturing, 18*(4), 495–512. https://doi.org/10.1016/S0883-9026(03)00057-0

Zahra, S. A. (2020). Technological capabilities and international expansion: The moderating role of family and non-family firms' social capital. *Asia Pacific Journal of Management, 37*(2), 391–415. https://doi.org/10.1007/s10490-018-9607-7

Zhou, L., Han, Y., & Gou, C. (2019). Influence of family involvement on family firm internationalization: The moderating effects of industrial and institutional environments. *Sustainability, 11*(20), 5721. https://doi.org/10.3390/su11205721

CHAPTER 3

The Choice Between Wholly Owned Subsidiaries and Joint Ventures Within Family Firms: A Theoretical Investigation from the Socioemotional Wealth Perspective

Abstract Recent applications of behavioral theories into the context of family-controlled firms assert a preference of family decision-makers for strategic actions that allow them Socioemotional Wealth (SEW) preservation, which ultimately means avoiding losing control of the firm. This chapter theoretically investigates how family control loss aversion drives family leaders' entry mode decisions and, more specifically, the choice between settling a wholly-owned subsidiary and a joint venture in the foreign country. The conceptual argumentation proposed suggests that that family leaders are either more or less willing to preserve family control—entering the foreign market through a wholly-owned subsidiary—depending on whether the firm is exposed to low or high performance and emotional hazards as well as high cultural distance between the domestic and the foreign country.

Keywords Family firms • Socioemotional wealth • Joint ventures • Wholly-owned subsidiaries • Cultural distance

---

The author is also Affiliate Researcher at IPAG Entrepreneurship & Family Business Center, IPAG Business School, France.

C. Pongelli, *Family Firms into International Markets*,
https://doi.org/10.1007/978-3-031-05398-6_3

3.1 The Socioemotional Wealth Perspective as a Theoretical Lens for Family Firms Internationalization

The study of all fundamental corporate strategic decisions has been traditionally informed by behavioral theories, according to which decision-makers show a preference for those actions that allow them to avoid a loss to their endowment, suggesting that risk bearing is subjective and depends on perceived threats to a decision makers' endowment (March & Shapira, 1987, 1992; Tversky & Kahneman, 1986; Wiseman & Gomez-Mejia, 1998). In the last 15 years, behavioral theories found their second youth in their pervasive application into the context of family firms. Moving from the seminal work by Gomez-Mejia et al. (2007), scholars started to argue the importance to investigate decision makers' attitudes in family firms. According to these interpretations, family decision-makers (family principals, most often acting in leadership positions) prove to be inherently loss adverse as to their regard of Socioemotional Wealth (SEW), i.e. the affective endowments or non-financial aspects of the family business.

Socioemotional wealth can be considered as a broad construct that comprises the non-financial rewards that family owners receive from their ownership position in the firm and that distinguish them from non-family principals (Gomez-Mejia et al., 2011). Preserving SEW has manifold dimensions which have a different salience within the family firm according to the specific characteristics of the firm (such as, for example, the different family involvement in the ownership, management and Board of Directors).

Berrone et al. (2012) developed the so-called FIBER framework to outline five main SEW dimensions: family control and influence (F), the identification of the family with the firm and the consequent care for reputation (I), the willingness to bind social ties (B), the emotional attachment of family members to the firm (E), and the need to Renew family bonds through dynastic succession (R). This chapter relies on the "*F*" dimension to theoretically investigate how the willingness to protect the family control and influences represents the key reference point for strategic decisions in family firms with a family member in leadership position (Berrone et al., 2012).

Building on the idea that preserving SEW is a key goal for family decision-makers and attaining this goal requires primarily to retain the firm's control—since ownership enables the family to realize its interest through the firm (Gomez-Mejia et al., 2007; Zellweger et al., 2012)—, scholars investigated the impact of SEW preservation on decisions such as environmental performance (Berrone et al., 2010), diversification strategies (Gomez-Mejia et al., 2010), IPO underpricing (Leitterstorf & Rau, 2014), international acquisition near the end of a CEO's career horizon (Strike et al., 2015), R&D investment decisions (Patel & Chrisman, 2014), and succession decisions (Calabrò et al., 2018), amongst others. All these studies implicitly or explicitly assumed that, for family principals, major managerial decisions are driven by the wish to avoid family control losses, even if achieving this goal might entail a higher financial risk or reduced performance.

Also in the context of internationalization, the willingness to preserve family control in international investments has been recognized as a crucial driver for family firms' decisions. For instance, Pongelli et al. (2016) found that family SMEs prefer embarking on non-cooperative entry modes to guarantee full control over international activities, also when internationalization has sourcing purposes (Pongelli et al., 2019). Similarly, Yamanoi and Asaba (2018) relied on the concept of SEW preservation and, more specifically on the family firms wish to regard their subsidiaries as their own properties intended to be passed down to descendants, to suggest that higher levels of family ownership are associated to a preference for greenfield investments (rather than acquisitions) and wholly-owned subsidiaries (rather than investments shared with an external partner). This idea is confirmed by Boellis and colleagues (Boellis et al., 2016), and later on by Mariotti et al. (2021), which showed that stronger SEW preservation in family owned and managed firms is associated to a higher propensity for greenfield investments. The divestment process of a subsidiary in a foreign country was also studied from the SEW perspective to explain why family CEOs compared to non-family ones are less likely to divest foreign subsidiaries with large affective endowments (Kim et al., 2019).

At the same time, a more fine-grained conceptualization of this scholarly debate suggests that family firms are not blindly driven towards a particular entry mode but rather adjust their risk preferences based on internal and external factors (Arrègle et al., 2021). This is in line with the recently developed *situational* approach of SEW according to which the aversion towards family control losses typical of family principals changes according to various circumstances, among whom the level of performance hazard is one of the most important (Calabrò et al., 2018;

Gomez-Mejia et al., 2007, 2010; Minichilli et al., 2016). This chapter confirms and expands this idea by focusing on family leaders' decisions on the subsidiary ownership choice, i.e. the choice between either setting up a wholly-owned subsidiary or forming a joint venture in a foreign country (Hennart & Larimo, 1998). More precisely, the aim is to understand the effect of family leaders' control loss aversion when performance and emotional hazards occur as well as when settling the subsidiary in a culturally distant country.

Entering foreign markets is in fact a key strategic decision that firms of every size and organizational type have sooner or later to face, and deciding the subsidiary ownership structure is one of the most relevant choices (e.g. Brouthers et al., 2003; Guillén, 2003; Hennart & Larimo, 1998; Makino & Neupert, 2000). It may become of paramount importance in family firms where the strategic ingredient of the subsidiary ownership choice is blended with emotional drivers of the family leaders' choices. Family leaders are especially sensitive to this strategic choice due to the '*exclusive*' versus the '*shared*' control that the corporate firm will have over the foreign investments, in the case, respectively, of a wholly-owned subsidiary as opposed to a joint venture (Pongelli et al., 2021a). Because the family control on the subsidiary can be considered as a prolongation of the family control on the parent company, the subsidiary ownership choice is an ideal context to investigate the family leaders risk preferences as their decisions trigger their loss aversion behavior. While prevailing SEW assumptions and recent empirical findings would suggest family leaders opting for a wholly-owned subsidiary to avoid a dilution in the family's control (Abdellatif et al., 2010; Gomez-Mejia et al., 2011; Pongelli et al., 2016, 2019, 2021a), this conceptual chapter aims to suggest that family firms' choices over the ownership structures of their subsidiaries cannot be generalized—like most of the other strategic decisions—and rather depend upon the occurrence of internal and external contingencies.

Accordingly, answering the following research questions might be particularly important in understanding how the family control loss aversion has a different intensity within family firms: *How does the level of performance hazard influence the strategic decision that family leaders make on subsidiary ownership policy? Also, how, does this decision vary when the performance hazard is coupled with emotional hazard and when the foreign country is culturally distant from the domestic one?*

As such, in the subsequent sections firstly it is explained how the level of performance hazard influences the family leaders' decision on the extent of control they want to keep in the subsidiary; secondly, it is proposed that this relation is either mitigated or reinforced depending on the level of emotional hazard. Finally the moderating role of the cultural distance between the domestic and the foreign market is discussed.

3.2 The Choice Between Wholly-Owned Subsidiary and Joint Venture

When establishing a subsidiary abroad, firms can start up new ventures or acquire existing ones (Brouthers & Brouthers, 2000). In both cases firms can set up a subsidiary which they own completely or form joint ventures with partners. This choice between a fully or only partially-owned affiliate is usually named in literature as subsidiary ownership policy and has received an uncommonly high attention by international business scholars. This attention is motivated by the several implications of ownership choice over a number of issues such as sourcing strategies, transfer pricing, integration of the firms' worldwide activities and ultimately, the subsidiary performance (Brouthers & Hennart, 2007; Erramilli, 1996).

Prior studies have extensively built on the transaction cost theory to explain the choice between wholly-owned subsidiary and joint venture (e.g. Brouthers et al., 2003; Guillén, 2003; Makino & Neupert, 2000), which suggests that a joint venture is preferred to a wholly-owned subsidiary when the investing firm needs to obtain complementary assets leveraging on a local partner. Other studies also emphasized the relevance of non-transaction cost factors such as host government restrictions, host country risk and uncertainty, firm nationality, as well as other strategic factors (Brouthers, 2013; Delios & Beamish, 1999; Gomes-Casseres, 1990; Hill et al., 1990). Indeed, subsidiary ownership policies could be a very complex function of numerous factors including host country, industry, product, and the firms' characteristics. A transaction cost perspective cannot always explain all the antecedents (Makino & Neupert, 2000), especially in the case of family firms. This does not mean that family business scholars cannot derive interesting insights from the transaction cost perspective, as is in the case of the study developed by Sestu and Majocchi (2020), where the authors used this theoretical approach to investigate the impact of family involvement on the choice between wholly-owned subsidiary and joint venture both from the investing firm and the local partner sides.

However, SEW is generally considered as the home-grown theoretical approach for the family business field in order to grasp the way family decision-makers manage internationalization.

It was found that due to their need to balance the business and the family demands and the consequent joint pursuit of economic and non-economic goals in international decisions (Pongelli et al., 2021b), how family decision-makers lead internationalization can be unique (Banalieva & Eddleston, 2011; Boellis et al., 2016; Pongelli et al., 2021a). According to previous studies, while family leaders carefully consider the economic consequences of their strategic decisions, non-economic consequences are often likely to play a major role (e.g. Gomez-Mejia et al., 2007, 2011). In other terms, in assessing the relative risk of various strategic choices, family leaders have an additional reference point compared to outside executives who have no emotional ties with the company, which is exactly the SEW preservation. SEW preservation is realized through family control maintenance, and family control loss aversion drives the family leader's choice even if alternatives would bring some business risk mitigation (Gomez-Mejia et al., 2007, 2010), or imply an economic gain (Leitterstorf & Rau, 2014). This behavioral logic was first explored by Gomez-Mejia et al. (2007), who provided evidence that Spanish family olive oil mills were less likely to join cooperatives, thus accepting higher business risk in order to avoid family control dilution. Later on, Gomez-Mejia et al. (2010) similarly demonstrated that family firms diversify less than non-family firms, since diversification threatens SEW and weakens family power and control.

Under this theoretical lens, the subsidiary ownership policy might be especially challenging since it entails a major decision choice about either preserving family control—and associated SEW—in a foreign country, or alternatively sharing it with an external partner. According to the SEW preservation logic, the strategic choice that better enables to maintain family control will prevail over alternative decisions (Gomez-Mejia et al., 2007, 2010): along this logic, it is reasonable to argue that family leaders' have a preference for wholly-owned subsidiaries. Choosing a wholly-owned subsidiary as the entry mode fits with the need that the family leaders have of exercising direct control over the foreign investment (Kao et al., 2013). Instead, cooperating with a foreign partner in a joint venture implies accepting external equity or sharing part of each other's knowledge or customer base which are generally unwelcome to family firms, even if—compared to non-family firms—they have a higher ability to govern them due to their extraordinary relational capabilities (Debellis et al.,

2021). Whereas the investing firm exerts both full and direct control over the foreign investment in a wholly-owned subsidiary, key strategic choices are made alongside with the foreign partner in a joint venture. Having full control over the foreign subsidiary (through a wholly-owned subsidiary) also means freedom in appointing managers and in involving the family members autonomously. Furthermore, it would guarantee within the company the arbitrariness to treat family members or family assets differently from non-family ones (Kano & Verbeke, 2018). On the contrary, a joint venture would offer less freedom to hire family members unilaterally as key managerial roles and their treatment would be negotiated between the partners (Yamanoi & Asaba, 2018).

However, a deeper understanding of SEW conceptualization suggests that family control loss aversion has a different intensity in driving family leaders behavior depending on circumstances surrounding strategic decisions (e.g., Gomez-Mejia et al., 2011; Minichilli et al., 2016; Calabrò et al., 2018). Alongside the same lines, a recent study by Kao and Kuo (2017) proposed that whether family firms are either more (or not) likely to choose full control FDIs over cooperative ones may vary depending on the level of the internal and external uncertainty they encounter. Indeed, business risk and SEW risk—which typically trade-off against each other—get aligned in driving strategic decisions when the level of uncertainty rises (Alessandri et al., 2018; Gomez-Mejia et al., 2018).

Following this logic, in the subsequent sections the aim is to understand whether the family leader's willingness to protect family control through a wholly-owned subsidiary varies based on the level of performance hazard, emotional hazard, and the cultural distance.

3.3 Family Control Loss Aversion and Performance Hazard

Performance hazard can be defined as "*the likelihood that bad things happen*" (Gomez-Mejia et al., 2007, p. 111) and represents the perceived negative consequences from a given choice (March & Shapira, 1987; Shapira, 1992). Performance hazard risk can itself be split into two dimensions, *probability of failure* as "*the worst case*" (Shapira, 1992, p. 135) and *below-target performance*. While the first type describes bankruptcy or default, the latter refers to the past or competitors' performance from the firms' perspective. Despite the two-fold meanings, in this chapter the term performance hazard is mainly used to refer to performance below target.

The idea that performance hazard influences the SEW preservation was first explored by the very same study that first introduced SEW (Gomez-Mejia et al., 2007). Subsequently, Gomez-Mejia et al. (2010) found that large publicly traded family firms have a higher propensity for diversification—thus accepting family control losses—as the firm performance decreases. More recently, Gomez-Mejia et al. (2018) showed that the likelihood for acquisitions—which are associated to high levels of risk for SEW preservation—increases as the firms' performance hazard increases. Hence, depending on whether firm performance is improving or declining, i.e. on the level of performance hazard, the SEW preservation will have a different intensity in driving strategic decisions (Gomez-Mejia et al., 2007, 2010). While family leaders will consider SEW preservation as an important reference point under a good performance trend, that their goal will have a lower emphasis when the firm is experiencing a performance hazard. The underlying logic is that SEW would be completely destroyed if the firm fails to survive, as "*…the relative utility of preserving SEW at the expenses of bearing higher business risk should decline accordingly.*" (Gomez-Mejia et al., 2010, p. 232). Or to put it differently, the family control loss aversion will have a different weight in driving the family leaders' decisions depending on the level of performance hazard. Along this line of reasoning, it is suggested that the choice joint venture vs. wholly-owned subsidiary for family leaders will depend on whether the family firm is experiencing a performance hazard or not. Hence, the idea is that a family leaders' behavior will switch from a high family control loss aversion to a low family control loss aversion as a substantial performance hazard steps in (Pongelli et al., 2021a).

In more detail, when the family firm investing abroad is suffering from low performance, the family leader will be less focused on non-economic goals (Gomez-Mejia et al., 2011), and thus is less adverse to dilute the family control through a joint venture: mitigating that performance hazard to safeguard SEW in a long-term perspective will be a priority. Since it allows to share business risk with an external party and restrains the investment (Brouthers & Hennart, 2007), a joint venture is supposed to be in line with that priority. On the contrary, when the family firm is experiencing positive performance, the family control loss aversion will play a pivotal role in driving the decision-maker towards a wholly-owned subsidiary, in order to keep the entire family control over the foreign investment.

Proposition 1

The level of performance hazard affects the family firms' subsidiary ownership choice: Under low performance hazard, the family leader will be more likely to choose a wholly-owned subsidiary, while under high performance hazard he/she will be more likely to choose joint venture.

3.4 Family Control Loss Aversion and Emotional Hazard

Family identity refers to the close identification of the family with the firm (Berrone et al., 2012; Gomez-Mejia et al., 2014). The family identity acts as a glue for family members, holding the group together under the common goal and also to the common pride of the fulfillment of the family firm obligations, so that the family and the organization are inextricably intermeshed (Dyer Jr & Whetten, 2006; Berrone et al., 2010; Zellweger et al., 2010, 2013). Kinship ties and a common history have the unique potential to build a robust family identity in family firms, and encourages family members to support family goals (Sundaramurthy & Kreiner, 2008; Zellweger et al., 2010).

The identity of family members within the family business is inseparably tied to the firm when it carries the family's name: it induces the firm to be seen as a prolongation of the family itself both by internal and external stakeholders (Berrone et al., 2010). When the family's name (typically the founder's name) corresponds to the company's name, the family is highly visible in the company and strongly associated to the business (Craig et al., 2008). Belenzon et al. (2017) name this phenomenon as "*eponymous firms*" and suggests that this type of organization usually has higher reputation costs. Similarly, Deephouse and Jaskiewicz (2013), relying on a sample of firms from eight countries with reputation rankings published by The Reputation Institute, showed that eponymous firms exhibit higher reputation rankings. Consistently with the idea of reputation concerns, Minichilli et al. (2021) recently demonstrated that eponymous firms are associated with higher financial reporting quality.

Overall, the underlying logic is that the higher the visibility of the family in the business, as in the case of identical family and company names, the more blurred are the boundaries between the family and the business (Zellweger et al., 2013), with the consequence that the firms' behavior will have a direct repercussion to the family. It is thus plausible to infer that high identity family firms face higher emotional hazard compared to low identity family firms as they have a lot at stake in terms of emotional entrenchment: as such, the family leader will be more sensitive to make strategic decisions in-line with the family's interests and in order to protect the family's endowment when facing high emotional hazard. Indeed, whether or not the family strives for a family identity should explain the family firm's pursuit of non-financial goals (Zellweger et al., 2013): the importance of SEW preservation arises from identity consideration and it is anchored by family members whose identity is bound to the organization (Berrone et al., 2010). Building on the idea that strategic behaviors in family firms may differ based on the family-specific focus on SEW preservation (DeTienne & Chirico, 2013), family control loss aversion can be considered higher for those family leaders operating in firms that exhibit a strong family identity, i.e. facing higher emotional hazard. Choosing a wholly-owned subsidiary would avoid any risk that the family firm gets exposed to unpredictable reputational threats depending on the JV partner's behavior. Hence, not coping with an external partner allows the family leader to protect more easily the reputation of the owning-family in the foreign context, and to avoid perils of misalignment that often arise in alliances (Balmer & Greyser, 2002).

Therefore, the emotional hazard stemming from family identity may either mitigate or reinforce the relationship between high or low performance hazard, and the related family leaders' lower or higher propensity for a wholly-owned subsidiary. As discussed above, low performance hazard will drive family leaders to choose consistently with their loss aversion attitude—i.e. selecting a wholly-owned subsidiary (Gomez-Mejia et al., 2010, 2011); and the SEW preservation tendency will be further reinforced in the presence of higher emotional hazard (i.e. in firms with identical family and company names). On the contrary, when the firm is experiencing a high performance hazard, non-economic goals are supposed to make way for economic considerations (Gomez-Mejia et al., 2010), with family control loss aversion no longer being the key priority: reduced emphasis on non-economic goals for firms experiencing performance hazard will be further reduced when it matches with a low level of emotional hazard, making the likelihood of a wholly-owned subsidiary even lower.

Proposition 2

The family leader has a stronger positive relation with the choice of a wholly-owned subsidiary when the firm is characterized by low performance hazard and high emotional hazard. At the opposite, the family leader has a stronger negative relation with the choice of a wholly-owned subsidiary when the firm is characterized by high performance hazard and low emotional hazard.

3.5 The Role of Cultural Distance

The last part of this conceptual investigation takes into consideration the moderating role of the cultural distance between the domestic and the foreign market. The concept of distance in international business goes beyond the mere geographical dimension and includes all those factors that make it difficult to understand the foreign environment. Among these factors, one of the most relevant is the distance between the national cultural characteristics of the domestic market and the foreign country (Beugelsdijk et al., 2018; Hennart & Larimo, 1998; Hofstede, 1980).[1]

Although prior studies do not have a common opinion on whether cultural distance enhances the propensity to choose wholly-owned subsidiaries rather than joint ventures (e.g. Anand & Delios, 1997; Chang & Rosenzweig, 2001; Pak & Park, 2004), extant literature concurs that cultural distance shapes the subsidiary ownership policy according to the idea that "*the cultural context helps to define profit potential and/or the risk associated with a specific market entry*" (Brouthers & Brouthers, 2000, p. 91). Cultural distance generates a big uncertainty for internationalizing firms

[1] Although cultural distance is the most commonly used type of distance to understand risk perceptions in host countries, the international business literature considers cross-national distance as a multidimensional construct. To get a wider comprehension of this phenomenon see Berry et al. (2010). Extending the work of Ghemawat (2001), the article by Berry et al. (2010) proposes the following nine dimensions of cross-national distance: *geographic* (great circle distance between geographic center of countries), *cultural* (differences in attitudes toward authority, trust, individuality, and importance of work and family), *economic* (differences in economic development, and macroeconomic characteristics), *financial* (differences in financial sector development), *political* (differences in political stability and democracy), *administrative* (differences in colonial ties, language, religion, and legal system), *demographic* (differences in demographic characteristics), *knowledge* (differences in patents and scientific production), *global connectedness* (differences in tourism and internet use).

because it involves differences in values, norms, and behaviors (Gomez-Mejia et al., 2010). Family firms entering foreign markets with high cultural distance may perceive their business as being more vulnerable in this context due to the higher liability of foreignness and outsidership they would face (López-Duarte & Vidal-Suárez, 2010; Johanson & Vahlne, 2009). The cultural distance between home and host countries generates constraints for foreign investors that want to operate in the host country, and enhances the unfamiliarity with the foreign context and its relevant network (Arora & Fosfuri, 2000; Hennart & Larimo, 1998). Such differences may pertain to the local culture as well as to the business culture and generate distinctive challenges that—if ignored—they may represent a challenge for internationalizing firms. A research conducted by Löhde et al. (2017) on German family firms entering into India and China reported some significant examples. In India, the presence of the caste system is a unique obstacle for foreign firms due to its implications on doing business and the creation of a working environment in that context (e.g. it is forbidden for people from higher castes to work with people from lower castes). In China, business is strongly influenced by trust-based influential relationships and networking activities which facilitate deals and have a strategic role with suppliers and customers as well as with financial and governmental institutions. Although challenging for foreign firms, this concept—known as "*guanxi*"—is the lifeblood of conducting business in China and cannot be neglected neither overestimated (e.g. key information may be wrongly disclosed because of a different understanding of being in a trustworthy relationship).

In the same line, Reuber (2016) suggested that family principals may perceive cultural distance as a "*destabilizing factor*" due to the higher need to adapt to the local context and the difficulties in replicating the family business in the foreign country (e.g. product adaptations, language, and cultural training). A greater cultural distance means that both the external uncertainty—associated with operating in a foreign market—and the internal uncertainty—associated with the relationship with a potential partner in a joint venture—is enhanced. According to Del Bosco and Bettinelli (2020) the decision to choose joint venture or to avoid it (choosing full control) in culturally distant countries is a function of the relative importance attributed by the family firm to these two sources of uncertainty and the perception of the associated risks.

The role of cultural distance might be especially complex for family leaders. It was previously argued that family leaders prefer wholly-owned subsidiaries over joint ventures as entry modes in a foreign country when facing low performance hazard and high emotional hazard. Entering into a culturally distant country may lead family leaders to revise such risk preference. Hence, cultural distance increases information processing demands and the need to depend on others outside the family to interpret the environment (Gomez-Mejia et al., 2010). Under this circumstance, cooperation can be seen as an opportunity to take advantage of the local partner's familiarity with the foreign countries' culture and gain unique access to local knowledge that would be impossible for the firm to get alone. At the same time, reputation concerns which arise from the strong emotional hazard may play a weaker role in a culturally distant context.

All in all, the emotional hazard also reflects the risk that the family faces in terms of reputation, image and social legitimacy, (which are all core concerns for family members (Berrone et al., 2010)). Family leaders usually live close to the local community and become well-known to individuals in the domestic context, therefore gaining personal and family non-economic advantage from their local relations in that community (Berrone et al., 2010). As such, they are likely to perceive external pressures also from a personal point-of-view: depending on the level of family identity, the family leader who is "*speaking for the firm*" (Miller et al., 2013) will be more or less sensitive about the image the family firm has externally (Zellweger et al., 2013). At the opposite, the family firm, its tradition, and its family system are instead usually mostly unknown in a foreign country. It is argued that family leaders might be less sensitive to reputation concerns potentially stemming from cooperation, especially if that country is culturally distant from the domestic one (Hennart & Larimo, 1998). As the cultural distance between the home and the host country increases, the role of emotional hazard to reinforce the SEW preservation tendency and the family control loss aversion weakens: in this context the family leader will be less likely to enter the foreign market through a wholly-owned subsidiary.

Proposition 3

When the firm is characterized by low performance hazard and high emotional hazard, the family leader will be less likely to enter a foreign market through a wholly-owned subsidiary as the cultural distance between the domestic and the foreign country increases.

3.6 Concluding Considerations

The theoretical investigation of this chapter intends to make a step forward in disentangling and testing the roots of behavioral theories, and particularly SEW—given the specific focus on family firms. Building on insights from prospect theory (Kahneman & Tversky, 1979), proponents of the behavioral agency model, or BAM (Wiseman & Gomez-Mejia, 1998), elaborated on the idea that decision-makers' risk preferences will be highly dependent on the positive or negative framing of problems, influencing decisions through the positive prospects (gain mode), or negative ones (loss mode) that characterize the context of the decision-making processes. With respect to this, this chapter theoretically expands the idea that risk evaluation is subjective and also contextual, rather than being solely based on economic evaluations that consider risks against the financial returns.

Nevertheless, while context-based risk assessment might be extended also to managerial decisions, regardless of the ownership structure of the firm (March & Shapira, 1987, 1992), and what this theoretical argumentation uniquely shows is the role of the emotional decision-making driver inside family firms. It was observed how the emotional hazard—stemming from family identity—can strengthen or weaken the SEW loss aversion of family leaders operating under different levels of performance hazard. The contention is that whether the family firm is exposed to high emotional hazard or not, the SEW preservation goal plays an either higher or lower role in driving the family leaders' strategic decisions in the foreign markets. Furthermore, it is proposed that this relationship is further challenged by the role of cultural distance, such that the higher the cultural distance the weaker the role of the emotional driver in family leaders' strategic decisions. Hence, the family leaders' aversion to lose family control—and the related SEW preservation goal—varies not only depending on the level of performance and emotional hazard under which the leader operates, but also based on the foreign cultural context wherein the family control has to be maintained.

In this way, on the one hand, this chapter theoretically challenges the widely acknowledged opinion that family firms are willing to jeopardize financial performance in order to protect their SEW; and on the other, it expands the idea that the decision-making reference point for family leaders drastically switches when there is a severe performance hazard. Indeed, from the conceptual standpoint, the contrasting forces characterizing different circumstances surrounding family leader's strategic decisions are addressed.

Moreover, this conceptual argumentation also responds to the call for more attention on the inherent heterogeneity within the universe of family firms to understand their international behavior. Specifically, it contributes to the ongoing academic debate on the sources of such heterogeneity and adds to studies which highlighted the influence over international decisions of different characteristics at the ownership and the management levels as well as the occurrence of either internal or external hazard to the family wealth.

To get a more comprehensive understanding of the different drivers of entry mode decisions in family firms, the subsequent chapter offers an empirical investigation on 3939 foreign subsidiaries run by 586 Italian family firms and investigates the influence of performance and emotional hazards as well as the role of cultural distance in their subsidiary ownership choice.

References

Abdellatif, M., Amann, B., & Jaussaud, J. (2010). Family versus nonfamily business: A comparison of international strategies. *Journal of Family Business Strategy, 1*(2), 108–116. https://doi.org/10.1016/j.jfbs.2010.04.004

Alessandri, T. M., Cerrato, D., & Eddleston, K. A. (2018). The mixed gamble of internationalization in family and nonfamily firms: The moderating role of organizational slack. *Global Strategy Journal, 8*(1), 46–72. https://doi.org/10.1002/gsj.1201

Anand, J., & Delios, A. (1997). Location specificity and the transferability of downstream assets to foreign subsidiaries. *Journal of International Business Studies, 28*(3), 579–603. https://doi.org/10.1057/palgrave.jibs.8490112

Arora, A., & Fosfuri, A. (2000). Wholly owned subsidiary versus technology licensing in the worldwide chemical industry. *Journal of International Business Studies, 31*(4), 555–572. https://doi.org/10.1057/palgrave.jibs.8490922

Arregle, J.-L., Chirico, F., Kano, L., Kundu, S. K., Majocchi, A., & Schulze, W. S. (2021). Family firm internationalization: Past research and an agenda for the future. *Journal of International Business Studies, 52*(6), 1159–1198. https://doi.org/10.1057/s41267-021-00425-2

Balmer, J. M., & Greyser, S. A. (2002). Managing the multiple identities of the corporation. *California Management Review, 44*(3), 72–86.

Banalieva, E. R., & Eddleston, K. A. (2011). Home-region focus and performance of family firms: The role of family vs non-family leaders. *Journal of International Business Studies, 42*(8), 1060–1072. https://doi.org/10.1057/jibs.2011.28

Belenzon, S., Chatterji, A. K., & Daley, B. (2017). Eponymous entrepreneurs. *American Economic Review, 107*(6), 1638–1655. https://doi.org/10.1257/aer.20141524

Berrone, P., Cruz, C., Gomez-Mejia, L. R., & Larraza-Kintana, M. (2010). Socioemotional wealth and corporate responses to institutional pressures: Do family-controlled firms pollute less? *Administrative Science Quarterly, 55*(1), 82–113. https://doi.org/10.2189/asqu.2010.55.1.82

Berrone, P., Cruz, C., & Gomez-Mejia, L. R. (2012). Socioemotional wealth in family firms theoretical dimensions, assessment approaches, and agenda for future research. *Family Business Review, 25*(3), 258–279. https://doi.org/10.1177/0894486511435355

Berry, H., Guillen, M. F., & Zhou, N. (2010). An institutional approach to cross-national distance. *Journal of International Business Studies, 41*(9), 1460–1480. https://doi.org/10.1057/jibs.2010.28

Beugelsdijk, S., Kostova, T., Kunst, V. E., Spadafora, E., & Van Essen, M. (2018). Cultural distance and firm internationalization: A meta-analytical review and theoretical implications. *Journal of Management, 44*(1), 89–130. https://doi.org/10.1177/0149206317729027

Boellis, A., Mariotti, S., Minichilli, A., & Piscitello, L. (2016). Family involvement and firms' establishment mode choice in foreign markets. *Journal of International Business Studies, 47*(8), 929–950. https://doi.org/10.1057/jibs.2016.23

Brouthers, K. D. (2013). A retrospective on: Institutional, cultural and transaction cost influences on entry mode choice and performance. *Journal of International Business Studies, 44*(1), 14–22. https://doi.org/10.1057/jibs.2012.23

Brouthers, K. D., & Brouthers, L. E. (2000). Acquisition or greenfield start-up? Institutional, cultural and transaction cost influences. *Strategic Management Journal, 21*(1), 89–97. https://doi.org/10.1002/(SICI)1097-0266(200001)21:1<89::AID-SMJ85>3.0.CO;2-8

Brouthers, K. D., & Hennart, J. F. (2007). Boundaries of the firm: Insights from international entry mode research. *Journal of Management, 33*(3), 395–425. https://doi.org/10.1177/0149206307300817

Brouthers, K. D., Brouthers, L. E., & Werner, S. (2003). Transaction cost-enhanced entry mode choices and firm performance. *Strategic Management Journal, 24*(12), 1239–1248. https://doi.org/10.1002/smj.362

Calabrò, A., Minichilli, A., Amore, M. D., & Brogi, M. (2018). The courage to choose! Primogeniture and leadership succession in family firms. *Strategic Management Journal, 39*(7), 2014–2035. https://doi.org/10.1002/smj.2760

Chang, S. J., & Rosenzweig, P. M. (2001). The choice of entry mode in sequential foreign direct investment. *Strategic Management Journal, 22*(8), 747–776. https://doi.org/10.1002/smj.168

Craig, J., Dibbrell, C., & Davis, P. S. (2008). Leveraging family-based brand identity to enhance firm competitiveness and performance in family businesses. *Journal of Small Business Management, 46*(3), 351–371.

Debellis, F., De Massis, A., Petruzzelli, A. M., Frattini, F., & Del Giudice, M. (2021). Strategic agility and international joint ventures: The willingness-ability paradox of family firms. *Journal of International Management, 27*(1), 100739. https://doi.org/10.1016/j.intman.2020.100739

Deephouse, D. L., & Jaskiewicz, P. (2013). Do family firms have better reputations than non-family firms? An integration of socioemotional wealth and social identity theories. *Journal of Management Studies, 50*(3), 337–360. https://doi.org/10.1111/joms.12015

Del Bosco, B., & Bettinelli, C. (2020). How do family SMEs control their investments abroad? The role of distance and family control. *Management International Review, 60*(1), 1–35. https://doi.org/10.1007/s11575-019-00406-6

Delios, A., & Beamish, P. W. (1999). Geographic scope, product diversification and the corporate performance of Japanese firms. *Strategic Management Journal, 20*(8), 711–728. https://doi.org/10.1002/(SICI)1097-0266(199908)20:8<711::AID-SMJ41>3.0.CO;2-8

DeTienne, D. R., & Chirico, F. (2013). Exit strategies in family firms: How socioemotional wealth drives the threshold of performance. *Entrepreneurship Theory and Practice, 37*(6), 1297–1318. https://doi.org/10.1111/etap.12067

Dyer, W. G., Jr., & Whetten, D. A. (2006). Family firms and social responsibility: Preliminary evidence from the S&P 500. *Entrepreneurship Theory and Practice, 30*(6), 785–802. https://doi.org/10.1111/j.1540-6520.2006.00151.x

Erramilli, M. K. (1996). Nationality and subsidiary ownership patterns in multinational corporations. *Journal of International Business Studies, 27*(2), 225–248. https://doi.org/10.1057/palgrave.jibs.8490133

Ghemawat, P. (2001). Distance still matters: The hard reality of global expansion. *Harvard Business Review, 79*(8), 137–147.

Gomes-Casseres, B. (1990). Firm ownership preferences and host government restrictions: An integrated approach. *Journal of International Business Studies, 21*(1), 1–22. https://doi.org/10.1057/palgrave.jibs.8490324

Gomez-Mejia, L. R., Haynes, K. T., Núñez-Nickel, M., Jacobson, K. J., & Moyano-Fuentes, J. (2007). Socioemotional wealth and business risks in family-controlled firms: Evidence from Spanish olive oil mills. *Administrative Science Quarterly, 52*(1), 106–137. https://doi.org/10.2189/asqu.52.1.106

Gomez-Mejia, L. R., Makri, M., & Kintana, M. L. (2010). Diversification decisions in family-controlled firms. *Journal of Management Studies, 47*(2), 223–252. https://doi.org/10.1111/j.1467-6486.2009.00889.x

Gomez-Mejia, L. R., Cruz, C., Berrone, P., & De Castro, J. (2011). The bind that ties: Socioemotional wealth preservation in family firms. *Academy of Management Annals, 5*(1), 653–707. https://doi.org/10.5465/19416520.2011.593320

Gomez-Mejia, L., Cruz, C., & Imperatore, C. (2014). Financial reporting and the protection of socioemotional wealth in family-controlled firms. *European Accounting Review, 23*(3), 387–402. https://doi.org/10.1080/09638180.2014.944420

Gomez-Mejia, L. R., Patel, P. C., & Zellweger, T. M. (2018). In the horns of the dilemma: Socioemotional wealth, financial wealth, and acquisitions in family firms. *Journal of Management, 44*(4), 1369–1397. https://doi.org/10.1177/0149206315614375

Guillén, M. F. (2003). Experience, imitation, and the sequence of foreign entry: Wholly owned and joint-venture manufacturing by South Korean firms and business groups in China, 1987–1995. *Journal of International Business Studies, 34*(2), 185–198. https://doi.org/10.1057/palgrave.jibs.8400016

Hennart, J. F., & Larimo, J. (1998). The impact of culture on the strategy of multinational enterprises: Does national origin affect ownership decisions? *Journal of International Business Studies, 29*(3), 515–538. https://doi.org/10.1057/palgrave.jibs.8490005

Hill, C. W., Hwang, P., & Kim, W. C. (1990). An eclectic theory of the choice of international entry mode. *Strategic Management Journal, 11*(2), 117–128. https://doi.org/10.1002/smj.4250110204

Hofstede, G. (1980). *Culture's consequences: International differences in work related values.* Sage.

Johanson, J., & Vahlne, J. E. (2009). The Uppsala internationalization process model revisited: From liability of foreignness to liability of outsidership. *Journal of International Business Studies, 40*(9), 1411–1431. https://doi.org/10.1057/jibs.2009.24

Kahneman, D., & Tversky, A. (1979). Prospect theory: An analysis of decision under risk. *Econometrica, 47*(2), 263–291.

Kano, L., & Verbeke, A. (2018). Family firm internationalization: Heritage assets and the impact of bifurcation bias. *Global Strategy Journal, 8*(1), 158–183. https://doi.org/10.1002/gsj.1186

Kao, M. S., & Kuo, A. (2017). The effect of uncertainty on FDI entry mode decisions: The influence of family ownership and involvement in the board of directors. *Journal of Family Business Strategy, 8*(4), 224–236. https://doi.org/10.1016/j.jfbs.2017.09.003

Kao, M. S., Kuo, A., & Chang, Y. C. (2013). How family control influences FDI entry mode choice. *Journal of Management & Organization, 19*(4), 367–385. https://doi.org/10.1017/jmo.2013.23

Kim, H., Hoskisson, R. E., & Zyung, J. D. (2019). Socioemotional favoritism: Evidence from foreign divestitures in family multinationals. *Organization Studies, 40*(6), 917–940. https://doi.org/10.1177/0170840619838955

Leitterstorf, M. P., & Rau, S. B. (2014). Socioemotional wealth and IPO underpricing of family firms. *Strategic Management Journal, 35*(5), 751–760. https://doi.org/10.1002/smj.2236

Löhde, A. S. K., Calabrò, A., & Campopiano, G. (2017). *Behavioral and cultural aspects of German family firms internationalizing to China and India.* Research report. https://www.deginvest.de/International-financing/DEG/Download-Center/Publikationen-mit-Partnern/

López-Duarte, C., & Vidal-Suárez, M. M. (2010). External uncertainty and entry mode choice: Cultural distance, political risk and language diversity. *International Business Review, 19*(6), 575–588. https://doi.org/10.1016/j.ibusrev.2010.03.007

Makino, S., & Neupert, K. E. (2000). National culture, transaction costs, and the choice between joint venture and wholly owned subsidiary. *Journal of International Business Studies, 31*(4), 705–713. https://doi.org/10.1057/palgrave.jibs.8490930

March, J. G., & Shapira, Z. (1987). Managerial perspectives on risk and risk taking. *Management Science, 33*(11), 1404–1418. https://doi.org/10.1287/mnsc.33.11.1404

March, J. G., & Shapira, Z. (1992). Variable risk preferences and the focus of attention. *Psychological Review, 99*(1), 172–183. https://doi.org/10.1037/0033-295X.99.1.172

Mariotti, S., Marzano, R., & Piscitello, L. (2021). The role of family firms' generational heterogeneity in the entry mode choice in foreign markets. *Journal of Business Research, 132*, 200–212. https://doi.org/10.1016/j.jbusres.2020.10.064

Miller, D., Minichilli, A., & Corbetta, G. (2013). Is family leadership always beneficial? *Strategic Management Journal, 34*(5), 553–571. https://doi.org/10.1002/smj.2024

Minichilli, A., Brogi, M., & Calabrò, A. (2016). Weathering the storm: Family ownership, governance, and performance through the financial and economic crisis. *Corporate Governance: An International Review, 24*(6), 552–568. https://doi.org/10.1111/corg.12125

Minichilli, A., Prencipe, A., Radhakrishnan, S., & Siciliano, G. (2021). What's in a name? Eponymous private firms and financial reporting quality. *Management Science, 68*(3), 2330–2348. https://doi.org/10.1287/mnsc.2021.3974

Pak, Y. S., & Park, Y. R. (2004). Global ownership strategy of Japanese multinational enterprises: A test of internalization theory. *Management International Review, 44*(1), 3–21.

Patel, P. C., & Chrisman, J. J. (2014). Risk abatement as a strategy for R&D investments in family firms. *Strategic Management Journal, 35*(4), 617–627. https://doi.org/10.1002/smj.2119

Pongelli, C., Caroli, M. G., & Cucculelli, M. (2016). Family business going abroad: The effect of family ownership on foreign market entry mode decisions. *Small Business Economics, 47*(3), 787–801. https://doi.org/10.1007/s11187-016-9763-4

Pongelli, C., Calabrò, A., & Basco, R. (2019). Family firms' international make-or-buy decisions: Captive offshoring, offshore outsourcing, and the role of home region focus. *Journal of Business Research, 103*, 596–606. https://doi.org/10.1016/j.jbusres.2018.02.033

Pongelli, C., Calabrò, A., Quarato, F., Minichilli, A., & Corbetta, G. (2021a). Out of the comfort zone! Family leaders' subsidiary ownership choices and the role of vulnerabilities. *Family Business Review, 34*(4), 404–424. https://doi.org/10.1177/08944865211050858

Pongelli, C., Valentino, A., Calabrò, A., & Caroli, M. (2021b). Family-centred goals, geographic focus and family firms' internationalization: A study on export performance. *Entrepreneurship & Regional Development, 33*(7–8), 580–598. https://doi.org/10.1080/08985626.2021.1925851

Reuber, A. R. (2016). An assemblage – Theoretic perspective on the internationalization processes of family firms. *Entrepreneurship Theory and Practice, 40*(6), 1269–1286. https://doi.org/10.1111/etap.12243

Sestu, M. C., & Majocchi, A. (2020). Family firms and the choice between wholly owned subsidiaries and joint ventures: A transaction costs perspective. *Entrepreneurship Theory and Practice, 44*(2), 211–232. https://doi.org/10.1177/1042258718797925

Shapira, Z. (1992). *Risk taking: A managerial perspective*. Russell Sage Foundation.

Strike, V. M., Berrone, P., Sapp, S. G., & Congiu, L. (2015). A socioemotional wealth approach to CEO career horizons in family firms. *Journal of Management Studies, 52*(4), 555–583. https://doi.org/10.1111/joms.12123

Sundaramurthy, C., & Kreiner, G. E. (2008). Governing by managing identity boundaries: The case of family businesses. *Entrepreneurship Theory and Practice, 32*(3), 415–436. https://doi.org/10.1111/j.1540-6520.2008.00234.x

Tversky, A., & Kahneman, D. (1986). Rational choice and the framing of decisions. *Journal of Business, 59*(4), 251–278.

Wiseman, R. M., & Gomez-Mejia, L. R. (1998). A behavioral agency model of managerial risk taking. *Academy of Management Review, 23*(1), 133–153. https://doi.org/10.5465/amr.1998.192967

Yamanoi, J., & Asaba, S. (2018). The impact of family ownership on establishment and ownership modes in foreign direct investment: The moderating role of corruption in host countries. *Global Strategy Journal, 8*(1), 106–135. https://doi.org/10.1002/gsj.1198

Zellweger, T. M., Eddleston, K. A., & Kellermanns, F. W. (2010). Exploring the concept of familiness: Introducing family firm identity. *Journal of Family Business Strategy, 1*(1), 54–63. https://doi.org/10.1016/j.jfbs.2009.12.003

Zellweger, T. M., Kellermanns, F. W., Chrisman, J. J., & Chua, J. H. (2012). Family control and family firm valuation by family CEOs: The importance of intentions for transgenerational control. *Organization Science, 23*(3), 51–868. https://doi.org/10.1287/orsc.1110.0665

Zellweger, T. M., Nason, R. S., Nordqvist, M., & Brush, C. G. (2013). Why do family firms strive for nonfinancial goals? An organizational identity perspective. *Entrepreneurship Theory and Practice, 37*(2), 229–248. https://doi.org/10.1111/j.1540-6520.2011.00466.x

CHAPTER 4

The Choice Between Wholly-Owned Subsidiaries and Joint Ventures Within Family Firms: An Empirical Analysis

Abstract This chapter provides an empirical analysis on the relationship between family leadership and entry mode decisions. Specifically, the analysis are based on a sample of 3939 foreign subsidiaries run by 586 family-controlled firms and aims at investigating trade-offs and interactions between performance and emotional hazards as drivers of the choice between wholly-owned subsidiary and joint venture in family led firms. Findings show that the family leader's willingness to preserve family control through a wholly-owned subsidiary is stronger when low performance hazard matches with high emotional hazard. Empirical evidence also indicates this tendency weakens as the cultural distance between the domestic and the foreign country increases.

Keywords Family firms • Socioemotional wealth • Joint ventures • Wholly-owned subsidiaries • Cultural distance

---

The author is also Affiliate Researcher at IPAG Entrepreneurship & Family Business Center, IPAG Business School, France.

C. Pongelli, *Family Firms into International Markets*,
https://doi.org/10.1007/978-3-031-05398-6_4

4.1 The Sample

This chapter aims to provide empirical evidence for the theoretical propositions included in Chap. 3. To improve the understanding of the inherent heterogeneity of family firms' entry mode decisions, the analyses included in this chapter intends to supply an empirical answer to the following questions: *How much does the presence of a family influence the choice between wholly-owned subsidiary and joint venture in family firms? How does this relationship change according to the different levels of performance and emotional hazard as well as cultural distance?*

This empirical investigation considers the foreign entry as the level of analysis and relies on a unique data set covering internationalized Italian family firms (i.e. that undertake at least one foreign direct investment) with more than 50 million of euros of revenues. The threshold of 50 million of euros of revenues allows considering only medium and large firms, thus assuring a high availability of information about both the firm and the foreign entry.

The data set is assembled using detailed and updated information from different sources. Firstly, accounting and financial data are retrieved from AIDA, the Italian branch of the Bureau van Dijk data provider. Then, the financial data was matched with governance information obtained from official public filings stored at the Italian Chamber of Commerce (Amore et al., 2014). Finally, data on foreign direct investments are gathered from the Reprint data set (Mariotti et al., 2015), that lists information on foreign entries undertaken by large Italian firms worldwide. These data are obtained from the companies' annual reports and crosschecked with press releases, newspapers and company websites. Information on individual characteristics come from sources such as the annual corporate governance report, the company website, the Italian Who's Who list of top executives, and articles from the specialized press (Minichilli et al., 2016. Furthermore, in line with international business literature (Cho & Padmanabhan, 1995; Hennart & Reddy, 1997; Padmanabhan & Cho, 1996), empirical analyses considered one single home country, in order to avoid biases due to the impact of home country national differences on the entry mode.

Following existing studies, family firms are defined according to the equity share that is held by family members that allows controlling the firm (Faccio & Lang, 2002; Anderson & Reeb, 2003). Since concentrated ownership structures are common in Italy, a stake of 50 percent is required to control the firm (Miller et al., 2013). However, if the parent firm is listed, the threshold for control is reduced to 25 percent of equity. With the selected criteria, the final sample consists of 3939 foreign entries run by 586 family firms, undertaken between 1995 and 2013 in 27 different countries.

4.2 The Variables

Dependent Variable

Wholly-owned subsidiary. Coherently with previous studies (Makino & Neupert, 2000; Brouthers, 2002), if the parent firm owns more than 95 percent of the equity's foreign subsidiary, we classify it as a wholly-owned subsidiary; otherwise, we consider it as a joint venture. Operationally, the dependent variable is a dummy that takes value 1 when the foreign entry is a wholly-owned subsidiary, and 0 when it is a joint venture.

Main Explanatory Variables

Family leader. When the family firm has a family leader, the variable takes value 1; otherwise, it is 0. The firm leader is defined as the individual who has been appointed as a CEO, executive president or leader without a formal board of directors (Miller et al., 2013; Boellis et al., 2016). Family members are those with blood or marital ties to the owning family, identified through surname affinity (Amore et al., 2014).

Cultural distance. Cultural distance is a widely employed concept in the international business literature. Nevertheless, some authors highlighted that cultural distance is affected by theoretical and empirical pitfalls (Shenkar, 2001; Avloniti & Filippaios, 2014). Specifically, one of the problems associated with the cultural distance measurement is due to the fact that it assumes stability over time, whilst cultures evolve and co-evolve (Shenkar, 2001). In order to remove this illusion of stability, this analysis relies on Berry et al. (2010) variables. Indeed, they employ the World Value Survey (Inglehart, 2004) to replicate Hofstede's (1980) uncertainty avoidance, power distance, individualism, and masculinity dimensions at specified intervals of time (i.e. three or four years). In such a way, it is possible to observe how cultural distances change over time. Finally, the four dimensions are grouped in a single index through the Mahalanobis calculation (De Maesschalck et al., 2000), because it is scale invariant and takes into account the variance-covariance matrix. Finally, values are standardized. More specifically:

$$\textit{Cultural distance} = \sqrt{\frac{1}{4}\sum_{i=1}^{4}\left(x_{i,j}-\mu_i\right)^T S^{-1}\left(x_{i,j}-\mu_i\right)}$$

where:

$x_{i,j}$ is the cultural distance for the i-th dimension between Italy and the j-th country;

μ_i is the mean distance for the i-th dimension of cultural distance;

S is the distances' variance-covariance matrix.

Control Variables

A set of variables is included in the econometric models to control for several determinants of the choice between wholly-owned subsidiary and joint venture and avoid potential endogeneity issues due to omitted variables. In particular, firm-level controls (that refer to the parent company) and country-level controls (that are specific of the host country of the foreign entry) are employed.

Firm-Level Controls

Parent age is the difference between the year of the foreign entry and the parent's foundation year. The former is retrieved from Reprint and the latter from AIDA—Bureau van Dijk. Older firms are more diversified and professionalized (Anderson & Reeb, 2003). As such, they are expected to possess more financial and managerial resources that would lower the need of having a partner, hence increasing the wholly-owned subsidiary propensity.

Parent size is measured with the number of employees recorded by the parent firm in the year of the investment. The value is log-transformed due to the right-skewed distribution. Data are taken from AIDA—Bureau van Dijk. As for age, size is a proxy of the presence of resources constituting a competitive advantage in international markets that would augment the probability of establishing wholly-owned subsidiaries (Filatotchev et al., 2007).

Leverage. Financial constraints may affect the subsidiary ownership policy as the lack of financial resource may hamper the equity stake held in the foreign firm (Miller et al., 2010). Then the lower leverage is expected to favor wholly-owned subsidiaries. The analysis controls for this aspect by considers the parent's leverage ratio. It is computed as the ratio between outstanding debt and equity. Data are taken from AIDA—Bureau van Dijk.

R&D intensity is the ratio between the R&D expenses and the total sales (Makino & Neupert, 2000). Data are log-transformed because of the right skewness of the distribution. It is a proxy of the firm's asset specificity. The higher the asset specificity, the higher the need to protect it, thus favoring wholly-owned subsidiaries. Data on R&D expenses and total sales come from the annual reports.

Family ownership. The power and pressure that the family leader may exercise over the family firm is strongly associated with the control that the family has at the ownership level. This aspect is measured through the percentage of family-controlled shares, a measure widely employed by previous studies also in the context of internationalization choices (e.g., Sciascia et al., 2012; Xu et al., 2020; Zahra, 2003). Data come from the Italian Chamber of Commerce.

First generation. The analysis also distinguishes among the family generations who run the family firm as it may influence the decision-making process (Gomez-Mejia et al., 2010). In particular, this variable discriminates family firms run by the first generation from those controlled by later generation. For the former, this variable takes value 1; the latter are codified by 0.

Female leader. Extant research showed that gender interactions have relevance in decision-making, with particular reference to family firms (Amore et al., 2014). For this reason, the analysis includes a dummy variable that takes the value of 1 when the leader is a female and 0 when the leader is a male.

Leader tenure. Leaders with long tenure are deemed to have stronger power over the firm and, thus, be able to leverage on their tenure to drive the firm's strategies towards their preferred ones. Given the importance of a career horizon in the field of international acquisitions (Strike et al., 2015), the analysis controls for this aspect by inserting the number of years that the individual has been running the family firms as a leader. Data comes from company reports, the Italian Chamber of Commerce, AIDA—Bureau van Dijk and Who's Who.

Industry dummies. A set of industry dummies to take out any industry-specific effects are included. Dummy variables are defined according to the 2-digit NACE classification.

Country-Level Controls

Country risk plays a central role in the choice of the subsidiary ownership. Indeed, it is reasonable to enter countries that are exposed to higher political risks with a partner, in order to share the country risk. This analysis relies on the classification developed by OECD (2015), which lists countries according to both a quantitative and a qualitative risk evaluation and then assigns a risk factor that ranges between 0 (lower risk) to 7 (higher risk).

Administrative distance accounts for differences in bureaucratic patterns due to colonial ties, language, religion, and the legal system (Berry et al., 2010). They rely on the colonizer-colonized relationship, common language between the home and the host country, common religion and, commonalities in legal systems (La Porta et al., 1999). The Mahalanobis distance is then calculated in order to create a single index. Values are standardized as for cultural distance. Specifically:

$$Administrative\ distance = \sqrt{\frac{1}{4}\sum_{l=1}^{4}\left(y_{l,j}-\pi_l\right)^T V^{-1}\left(y_{l,j}-\pi_l\right)}$$

where:

$y_{l,j}$ is the administrative distance for the l-th dimension between Italy and the j-th country;

π_l is the mean distance for the l-th dimension of administrative distance;

V is the distances' variance-covariance matrix.

Geographic distance is the great circle distance between Italy and the foreign countrys' capitals. It takes account of transportation costs, time zones, and the like. It is retrieved from the Wharton database by Berry et al. (2010) and expressed in thousands of kilometers.

Time dummies. To control for time-specific contingencies that affect the subsidiary ownership policy, three time dummies are introduced. Specifically, since information for some data on the exact foreign entry year is missing, the analysis distinguishes between foreign entries that run between 1995–2000, 2001–2007, and 2008–2013. As such, it was always possible to assign every observation to these time spans.

4.3 The Model

The dependent variable *wholly-owned subsidiary* is dichotomous, thus the analysis employs probit models to analyze the impact of the aforementioned regressors on the likelihood of choosing a wholly-owned subsidiary rather than a joint venture. However, since most of the firms run more than one foreign entry, correlation among observations from the same company are allowed in order to relax the assumption of independence across observations. Consequently, standard errors are clustered at the firm level and the sample has the structure of a repeated cross-section. The possibility to use panel models was excluded because the same firm may run some foreign entries in one year and not in other years (Cameron & Trivedi, 2005).

In order to test the propositions described in Chap. 3, the models are run on the theoretically relevant sub-samples. This method brings two advantages compared to interact the variables. Firstly, it allows the controls to vary freely across the sub-sample, whilst employing a single model with interactions would tacitly assume that the controls have the same impact on the different categories. Secondly, since several dimensions are included in the analyses—i.e. family leader, cultural distance, and two hazard types (performance and emotional)—the number of interactions would be difficult to interpret. The sub-samples are generated along two dimensions: (i) performance hazard and (ii) emotional hazard. With respect to the first dimension, performance hazard represents the extent to which the performance of the firm is improving or declining (Gomez-Mejia et al., 2010). It is then calculated as one minus the natural logarithm of the ratio of firm performance (in terms of ROA) at time t and at time t-1. Finally, the analysis discriminates between firms with low performance hazard (i.e. firm's performance is improving) and high performance hazard (i.e. firm's performance is stable or declining). Instead, with respect to the second dimension, the analysis discriminates firms with high emotional hazard (i.e. when the family name is present in the company name—e.g. Barilla, Benetton or Ferragamo) and low emotional hazard (i.e. when the company name differs from the family name—e.g. Mediaset with the Berlusconi family and Brembo with the Bombassei family).

4.4 Findings Description

Table 4.1 provides the geographical distribution of the foreign entries and the average foreign entry per firm. Moreover, to show a clear picture of the sample distribution, two potential issues are addressed. Firstly, there could be countries that exhibit frequencies that are not economically driven. If this was the case, the estimates could present selection biases and underestimate the real economic drivers of the subsidiary ownership policies. Secondly, it is considered whether family and non-family leaders show divergences in the host country selection, since it would be worth investigating the reasons in order to avoid biasing the results. With

Table 4.1 Foreign entries statistics and geographic distribution

Country	*Non-family led*		*Family led*		*Total*	
	No.	*%*	*No.*	*%*	*No.*	*%*
China	283	18.42	509	21.18	792	20.11
United States	348	22.66	387	16.10	735	18.66
Germany	129	8.40	312	12.98	441	11.20
Spain	134	8.72	224	9.32	358	9.09
Brazil	96	6.25	120	4.99	216	5.48
Poland	53	3.45	95	3.95	148	3.76
Romania	37	2.41	111	4.62	148	3.76
India	51	3.32	85	3.54	136	3.45
Russia	42	2.73	73	3.04	115	2.92
Mexico	44	2.86	66	2.75	110	2.79
Argentina	41	2.67	59	2.46	100	2.54
Canada	51	3.32	46	1.91	97	2.46
Turkey	43	2.80	46	1.91	89	2.26
Australia	33	2.15	28	1.17	61	1.55
South Africa	15	0.98	44	1.83	59	1.50
Japan	24	1.56	30	1.25	54	1.37
Sweden	23	1.50	30	1.25	53	1.35
Bulgaria	11	0.72	24	1.00	35	0.89
Egypt	13	0.85	21	0.87	34	0.86
Morocco	11	0.72	21	0.87	32	0.81
Chile	18	1.17	13	0.54	31	0.79
Ukraine	8	0.52	22	0.92	30	0.76
South Korea	8	0.52	11	0.46	19	0.48
Finland	6	0.39	11	0.46	17	0.43
Norway	8	0.52	6	0.25	14	0.36
Indonesia	5	0.33	8	0.33	13	0.33
Jordan	1	0.07	1	0.04	2	0.05
Total foreign entries	1536	39.00	2403	61.00	3939	100.00
Number of firms	125	21.33	461	78.67	586	100.00
Average foreign entry per firm	12.29		5.21		6.72	

Note: Percentages in rows "Total foreign entries" and "Number of firms" are computed with reference to the "Total" column

reference to the first point, it is possible to note that the three most entered countries are China, the United States and Germany, which are the main Asian, American and European economies, respectively. In particular, 49.97 percent of the foreign entries in the sample have these countries as their destinations; according to the World Bank, the same countries account for the 40.62 percent of the World GDP in 2014. Furthermore, looking at the other countries, none of them is significantly over/underestimated with regard to its economics relevance and the economic relations with Italy. Moving to the preferences between family and non-family led firms, there is little variance by country. Specifically, the country where the discrepancy is the highest is the United States where—although total foreign entries in this country account for the 18.66 percent of the cases—family led firms show a 16.10 percent. Such a variance could be considered as physiological.

With regard to the number of foreign entries and firms, at a first glance, family led firms overcome their non-family counterparts in terms of foreign entries (2403 vs. 1536). However, the average foreign entry per firm is computed, it is possible to note that the former run 5.21 foreign entry per firm, while the latter reach a mean of 12.29. This result is consistent with previous studies that relate higher level of family involvement with lower level of international diversification and activity (Banalieva & Eddleston, 2011; Gomez-Mejia et al., 2010).

Table 4.2 reports the descriptive statistics of the variables, jointly with the pairwise correlations. It is observed that family firms opt for wholly-owned subsidiaries in 74.7 percent of the foreign entries. This finding is consistent with analogous studies that employed the same thresholds of 95 percent to distinguish between wholly-owned subsidiaries and joint ventures. Indeed, Brouthers (2002) finds that the 70 percent of the foreign entries are wholly-owned subsidiaries; Hennart et al. (2015) reported that 84 percent of foreign entries are wholly-owned subsidiaries. The parent age mean is equal to 43.8 years, but standard deviation is quite high, since our sample ranges from newly established ventures to more than a century old companies. Mean leverage has a value of 3.884. However, leverage can vary massively (the standard deviation is 3.642), as it often relies on firm and industry peculiarities, according to the corporate capital structure theory (Leary & Roberts, 2014). Further, families have a tight control on the family firms (77.1 percent of the equity on average). This is not surprising due to the high threshold selected to identify family control in such a concentrated market for corporate control as Italy is. Moreover, 46.3 percent of the investments come from family firms controlled by family members in the first generation. Finally, in spite of the mean leader tenure of 12 years, the highest tenure reaches 49 years. Although it may seem a long period, it refers to the founder of a family firm, who holds the role of CEO since the firm's inception.

Table 4.2 Descriptive statistics

#	*Variable*	*(1)*	*(2)*	*(3)*	*(4)*	*(5)*	*(6)*	*(7)*	*(8)*	*(9)*	*(10)*	*(11)*	*(12)*	*(13)*	*(14)*	*VIF*
(1)	Wholly-owned subsidiary															
(2)	Family leader	-0.063														1.341
(3)	Cultural distance	0.063	0.011													1.208
(4)	Parent age	0.073	-0.180	-0.067												2.264
(5)	Parent size	0.109	-0.362	-0.025	0.575											2.064
(6)	Leverage	-0.020	-0.115	-0.013	0.049	0.144										1.083
(7)	R&D intensity	0.083	-0.290	-0.011	0.456	0.506	0.158									1.597
(8)	Family ownership	-0.112	0.359	-0.009	-0.430	-0.564	-0.057	-0.488								1.737
(9)	First generation	0.025	0.031	0.034	-0.536	-0.175	-0.039	-0.190	0.137							1.475
(10)	Female leader	-0.018	0.183	-0.006	-0.129	-0.118	0.127	-0.101	0.170	0.116						1.111
(11)	Tenure leader	-0.049	0.285	0.025	-0.094	-0.174	-0.130	-0.047	0.226	-0.014	-0.081					1.169
(12)	Country risk	-0.016	-0.046	0.090	0.012	-0.026	0.031	-0.012	0.019	-0.017	0.026	-0.005				1.021
(13)	Admini-strative distance	-0.002	0.012	0.049	-0.026	-0.034	-0.019	-0.043	0.057	-0.011	0.025	0.016	0.048			1.011
(14)	Geographic distance	-0.018	-0.085	0.398	-0.020	0.041	0.004	0.078	-0.025	0.004	0.014	0.019	0.080	-0.012		1.227
	Mean	0.747	0.610	-0.003	43.839	7.641	3.884	0.009	0.771	0.463	0.058	12.056	5.041	-0.003	6.086	1.407
	Standard deviation	0.435	0.488	0.983	33.306	2.343	3.642	0.020	0.256	0.499	0.234	8.411	3.013	0.992	3.761	
	Minimum	0	0	-1.148	0	0.693	0	0	0	0	0	0	0	-1.063	0.954	
	Maximum	1	1	2.417	147	12.231	9.640	0.070	1	1	1	49	7	11.360	14.425	

Notes: Correlations of |0.031| or higher are significant at $p < 0.05$

Correlations of |0.041| or higher are significant at $p < 0.01$

Moving to the correlations, it is possible to observe that, despite a few exceptions, they are at moderate levels. When correlation seems high—in absolute terms—it should not cause concern. For instance, the largest value is -0.564, the correlation between family control and parent size. It seems reasonable that when a firm grows, it requires to finance such a growth and the family may not be able to face it, thus diluting control. However, to chase all doubts away, the variance inflator factor (VIF) is computed. Results may suffer of multicollinearity if such a factor exceeds 10 for any single variable or if the mean VIF is higher than 6 (Hair et al., 2009). Results are far from such thresholds, since the maximum VIF is 2.264 for parent size and the mean VIF is equal to 1.407.

Panels A and B of Table 4.3 provide a rough approximation of the *wholly-owned subsidiary* distribution, conditional to the performance and emotional hazards, for family and non-family managed firms, respectively. Regardless of the family identity, family leaders of firms with high performance hazard run less wholly-owned subsidiaries (67.60 percent) than

Table 4.3 Wholly-owned subsidiary propensity for family and non-family led firms

Panel A. Family led firms

		High EH (%)	*Low EH (%)*	*Difference (%)*
		77.50	69.86	7.64***
Low PH (%)	78.49	84.24	74.02	10.22***
High PH (%)	67.60	68.90	67.09	1.81
Difference (%)	10.89***	15.34***	6.93*	

Panel B. Non-family led firms

		High EH (%)	*Low EH (%)*	*Difference (%)*
		71.32	79.50	8.18**
Low PH (%)	76.50	66.10	78.39	12.29*
High PH (%)	78.66	72.86	79.87	7.01*
Difference (%)	2.16	6.76	1.48	

Notes:

PH performance hazard, *EH* emotional hazard

Differences are in absolute value

Significances refer to the two-tailed *t*-test

†$p < 0.10$, *$p < 0.05$, **$p < 0.01$, ***$p < 0.001$

their counterparts with a low performance hazard (78.49 percent). The difference is highly significant and in the same direction of Proposition 1. When experiencing a high performance hazard, family leaders are less averse to share the subsidiary's control with a partner. If this result is compared with the non-family leaders in panel B, it is possible to observe that the joint venture propensity difference between high and low performance hazard is negligible and not significant; therefore, in line with predictions of Chap. 3, the Socioemotional Wealth (SEW) preservation by family leaders becomes less relevant for firms with high performance hazard. Moreover, Proposition 2 suggests that family leaders prefer avoiding having a partner when emotional hazard is high. Indeed, regardless of the performance hazard, family leaders opt for wholly-owned subsidiaries in the 77.50 percent of cases when emotional hazard is high and 69.92 percent when it is low. Again, the difference is strongly significant. On the other hand, non-family leaders behave differently with regard to emotional hazard. In particular, given the lower stock of family-related endowment, it arises that they counter-balance the preference to retain control over the subsidiary. By examining the four combinations of performance and emotional hazards, it clearly emerges that there are two opposite focal points. Having said that, firms with low performance hazard share with those with high emotional hazard the preference for wholly-owned subsidiaries, it is reasonable that those firms that combine the two characteristics report the highest ratio of wholly-owned subsidiaries (84.24 percent). These firms undertake more wholly-owned subsidiaries than those with whom share the same level of emotional hazard, but not the same level of performance hazard (68.90 percent). The same is true with reference to those that have low performance hazard too, but low emotional hazard (74.02 percent). Each difference is statistically significant. On the opposite corner of the table, we have those firms whose hazards' levels hamper wholly-owned subsidiaries—i.e. they have high performance hazard and low emotional hazard. As a result, these firms report the lowest probability to opt for a wholly-owned subsidiary (67.09 percent). However, the difference with the firms with whom share one hazard is statistically weak (if they report the same level of emotional hazard identity) or negligible (if they report the same level of performance hazard). For the sake of brevity, with respect to the combination in non-family led firms in panel B, it is simply noted that, the statistics are symmetrical to those of family led firms.[1]

[1] Non-family leaders report specular preferences compared to the family ones. In particular, they show the highest propensity for wholly-owned subsidiary when the firm has high

As a preliminary analysis, it is tested whether family leaders favor or hinder internationalization. To do so, the whole population of large Italian family firms (both internationalized and active only domestically) is considered and a dummy variable—that it is equal to 1 if the firm has run at least one investment abroad and 0 otherwise—is included. Then the analysis regresses this dummy on the family leader variable and findings show that family led firms are only 1.4 percent less likely to invest abroad. However, the effect is not significant at any generally accepted significance level,[2] thus it is possible to infer that family led firms do not have a different propensity to invest abroad compared to their counterparts.

Econometric analyses are organized as follows. Table 4.4 reports the econometric estimates for the full sample and the two sub-samples distinguishing between high and low levels of performance hazard. Strictly related, Table 4.5 reports the average marginal effects[3] for the same models. Analogously, Table 4.6 reports the estimates for high and low identity firms, while Table 4.7 incorporates the average marginal effects. Finally, Table 4.8 and Table 4.9 show the estimates and average marginal effects, respectively, of the four possible combinations of performance mode and identity status.

performance hazard and low emotional hazard (79.87 percent). On the contrary, when the firm has low performance hazard and it has high emotional hazard, they show a weaker preference for wholly-owned subsidiary (66.10 percent). Furthermore, the differences along the quarters are rarely significant; therefore, the findings are driven mainly by the family leaders' behaviour, rather than from their non-family counterparts.

[2] The analyses are replicated by considering several control variables that could affect the decision to internationalize, which are the parent size, parent age, leverage, and R&D intensity. However, the impact of the family leader on internationalization is always negligible and never significant.

[3] For floating variables (i.e. parent age, leverage, family ownership, tenure leader, country risk, geographical distance), average marginal effects have to be interpreted as the average increase (decrease) in probability to run a wholly-owned subsidiary—compared to undertaking a joint venture—due to a unitary increase (decrease) of the independent variable. For standardized variables (i.e. cultural distance and administrative distance), average marginal effects refer to the average impact on the dependent variable of a one standard deviation variation, rather than a unitary change. For dummy variables (i.e. family leader, first generation, and female leader), they are the difference between the presence and absence of the condition indicated by the dummy. Finally, for log-transformed variables (i.e. parent age and R&D intensity), average marginal effects have to be interpreted as semi-elasticities, that is the average effect on the wholly-owned subsidiary probability of one percent change of the independent variable.

Table 4.4 Probit models. Dependent variable: WOS. Sample: Full, Low performance hazard and High performance hazard

	(1)	*(2)*	*(3)*	*(4)*	*(5)*	*(6)*
	Full sample	Full sample	Low PH	Low PH	High PH	High PH
Family leader		-0.039		**0.426***		**-0.310***
		(0.096)		**(0.182)**		**(0.127)**
Parent age	0.000	0.000	0.004	0.004	0.000	-0.000
	(0.002)	(0.002)	(0.003)	(0.003)	(0.002)	(0.002)
Parent size	0.096**	0.094**	0.099	0.081	0.094*	0.067†
	(0.030)	(0.030)	(0.067)	(0.067)	(0.037)	(0.035)
Leverage	-0.005	-0.005	-0.039†	-0.036†	0.009	0.011
	(0.009)	(0.009)	(0.021)	(0.021)	(0.009)	(0.009)
R&D intensity	0.892	0.767	-2.684	-0.633	2.080	2.324
	(2.205)	(2.171)	(6.652)	(6.227)	(3.038)	(2.939)
Family ownership	-0.120	-0.112	0.199	0.362	-0.043	0.072
	(0.195)	(0.199)	(0.396)	(0.373)	(0.226)	(0.236)
First generation	0.174*	0.173†	0.236	0.257	0.133	0.100
	(0.089)	(0.088)	(0.162)	(0.162)	(0.108)	(0.105)
Female leader	-0.048	-0.037	0.328	0.272	-0.111	0.012
	(0.121)	(0.124)	(0.275)	(0.265)	(0.162)	(0.177)
Tenure leader	-0.006	-0.005	-0.013†	-0.016*	-0.001	0.005
	(0.004)	(0.005)	(0.008)	(0.008)	(0.006)	(0.006)
Country risk	0.007	0.007	0.030*	0.029†	-0.001	-0.002
	(0.009)	(0.009)	(0.015)	(0.015)	(0.012)	(0.012)
Administrative distance	0.002	0.002	-0.008	-0.010	-0.010	-0.016
	(0.023)	(0.023)	(0.032)	(0.032)	(0.033)	(0.033)
Geographic distance	-0.006	-0.006	-0.014	-0.013	-0.004	-0.003
	(0.007)	(0.007)	(0.011)	(0.011)	(0.009)	(0.009)
Constant	-0.391	-0.370	-0.913	-1.260†	-0.164	0.038
	(0.380)	(0.389)	(0.759)	(0.724)	(0.461)	(0.457)
Industry dummies	Yes	Yes	Yes	Yes	Yes	Yes
Time dummies	Yes	Yes	Yes	Yes	Yes	Yes
Observations	3939	3939	1471	1471	2468	2468
Firms	586	586	204	204	382	382
Ratio of correct classification	74.61%	74.71%	78.45%	78.79%	73.18%	73.91%
Pseudo R^2	0.121	0.121	0.213	0.222	0.115	0.122
Likelihood ratio	335.52***	335.91***	220.29***	229.37***	204.72***	217.22***

Notes:

PH performance hazard

Firm-level clustered standard errors in parentheses

†$p < 0.10$, *$p < 0.05$, **$p < 0.01$, ***$p < 0.001$

Pseudo R^2 follows the Cragg & Uhler's calculation

Table 4.5 Average marginal effects. Dependent variable: WOS. Sample: Full, Low performance hazard and High performance hazard

	(1)	*(2)*	*(3)*	*(4)*	*(5)*	*(6)*
	Full sample	Full sample	Low PH	Low PH	High PH	High PH
Family leader		-0.011		**0.107***		**-0.095***
		(0.028)		**(0.046)**		**(0.039)**
Parent age	0.000	0.000	0.001	0.001	0.000	0.000
	(0.001)	(0.001)	(0.001)	(0.001)	(0.001)	(0.001)
Parent size	0.028**	0.028**	0.025	0.020	0.029**	0.021†
	(0.009)	(0.009)	(0.017)	(0.017)	(0.011)	(0.011)
Leverage	-0.002	-0.002	-0.010†	-0.009†	0.003	0.003
	(0.003)	(0.003)	(0.005)	(0.005)	(0.003)	(0.003)
R&D intensity	0.263	0.226	-0.681	-0.159	0.639	0.711
	(0.651)	(0.640)	(1.687)	(1.569)	(0.934)	(0.900)
Family ownership	-0.035	-0.033	0.051	0.091	-0.013	0.022
	(0.057)	(0.059)	(0.100)	(0.094)	(0.069)	(0.072)
First generation	0.051†	0.051†	0.060	0.065	0.041	0.030
	(0.026)	(0.026)	(0.041)	(0.041)	(0.033)	(0.032)
Female leader	-0.014	-0.011	0.083	0.069	-0.034	0.004
	(0.036)	(0.037)	(0.069)	(0.067)	(0.050)	(0.054)
Tenure leader	-0.002	-0.002	-0.003†	-0.004*	-0.000	0.001
	(0.001)	(0.001)	(0.002)	(0.002)	(0.002)	(0.002)
Country risk	0.002	0.002	0.008*	0.007†	-0.000	-0.001
	(0.003)	(0.003)	(0.004)	(0.004)	(0.004)	(0.004)
Administrative distance	0.001	0.001	-0.002	-0.002	-0.003	-0.005
	(0.007)	(0.007)	(0.008)	(0.008)	(0.010)	(0.010)
Geographic distance	-0.002	-0.002	-0.004	-0.003	-0.001	-0.001
	(0.002)	(0.002)	(0.003)	(0.003)	(0.003)	(0.003)
Industry dummies	Yes	Yes	Yes	Yes	Yes	Yes
Time dummies	Yes	Yes	Yes	Yes	Yes	Yes
Observations	3939	3939	1471	1471	2468	2468

Notes:

PH performance hazard

Robust standard errors in parentheses

†$p < 0.10$, *$p < 0.05$, **$p < 0.01$, ***$p < 0.001$

Table 4.6 Probit models. Dependent variable: WOS. Sample: High emotional hazard and Low emotional hazard

	(1)	(2)	(3)	(4)
	High EH	High EH	Low EH	Low EH
Family leader		**0.369***		**-0.282***
		(0.146)		**(0.121)**
Parent age	0.004	0.006	0.002	0.002
	(0.004)	(0.004)	(0.002)	(0.002)
Parent size	0.182**	0.188***	0.039***	0.050***
	(0.057)	(0.056)	(0.111)	(0.012)
Leverage	0.027	0.029	-0.007	-0.009
	(0.021)	(0.021)	(0.008)	(0.008)
R&D intensity	3.733	2.142	2.787	1.527
	(7.621)	(7.785)	(2.767)	(2.359)
Family ownership	-0.415	-0.340	-0.418†	-0.330
	(0.617)	(0.568)	(0.220)	(0.230)
First generation	0.317†	0.340†	0.156	0.145
	(0.182)	(0.177)	(0.111)	(0.106)
Female leader	0.021	-0.113	-0.039	0.027
	(0.207)	(0.210)	(0.129)	(0.135)
Tenure leader	-0.004	-0.009	-0.001	0.004
	(0.006)	(0.007)	(0.006)	(0.006)
Country risk	-0.009	-0.009	0.000	-0.000
	(0.017)	(0.017)	(0.011)	(0.011)
Administrative distance	-0.057	-0.051	0.010	0.009
	(0.040)	(0.040)	(0.027)	(0.027)
Geographic distance	0.013	0.015	0.011	0.010
	(0.014)	(0.014)	(0.008)	(0.008)
Constant	-1.123	-1.589*	0.448	0.551†
	(0.814)	(0.807)	(0.307)	(0.301)
Industry dummies	Yes	Yes	Yes	Yes
Time dummies	Yes	Yes	Yes	Yes
Observations	1107	1107	2832	2832
Firms	175	175	411	411
Ratio of correct classification	75.69%	75.69%	74.59%	74.59%
Pseudo R^2	0.163	0.177	0.083	0.092
Likelihood ratio	126.16***	137.43***	165.08***	183.51***

Notes:

EH emotional hazard

Firm-level clustered standard errors in parentheses

†$p < 0.10$, *$p < 0.05$, **$p < 0.01$, ***$p < 0.001$

Pseudo R^2 follows the Cragg & Uhler's calculation

Table 4.7 Average marginal effects. Dependent variable: WOS. Sample: High emotional hazard and Low emotional hazard

	(1)	*(2)*	*(3)*	*(4)*
	High EH	High EH	Low EH	Low EH
Family leader		**0.102****		**-0.086***
		(0.038)		**(0.036)**
Parent age	0.001	0.002	0.001	0.001
	(0.001)	(0.001)	(0.001)	(0.001)
Parent size	0.051***	0.052***	0.000***	0.000***
	(0.015)	(0.015)	(0.000)	(0.000)
Leverage	0.008	0.008	-0.002	-0.003
	(0.006)	(0.006)	(0.002)	(0.002)
R&D intensity	1.039	0.590	0.852	0.464
	(2.132)	(2.150)	(0.850)	(0.721)
Family ownership	-0.116	-0.094	-0.128†	-0.100
	(0.167)	(0.154)	(0.066)	(0.069)
First generation	0.088†	0.094†	0.048	0.044
	(0.049)	(0.048)	(0.034)	(0.032)
Female leader	0.006	-0.031	-0.012	0.008
	(0.058)	(0.057)	(0.039)	(0.041)
Tenure leader	-0.001	-0.002	-0.000	0.001
	(0.002)	(0.002)	(0.002)	(0.002)
Country risk	-0.003	-0.002	0.000	-0.000
	(0.005)	(0.005)	(0.003)	(0.003)
Administrative distance	-0.016	-0.014	0.003	0.003
	(0.011)	(0.011)	(0.008)	(0.008)
Geographic distance	0.004	0.004	0.003	0.003
	(0.004)	(0.004)	(0.002)	(0.002)
Industry dummies	Yes	Yes	Yes	Yes
Time dummies	Yes	Yes	Yes	Yes
Observations	1107	1107	2832	2832

Notes:

EH emotional hazard

Robust standard errors in parentheses

†$p < 0.10$, *$p < 0.05$, **$p < 0.01$, ***$p < 0.001$

Firstly, the effect of some relevant control variables is analyzed. Parent age and size, when significant, have positive signs in every table. It confirms the expectation that, *ceteris paribus*, older and larger firms have managerial and financial resources to follow a strategy based on wholly-owned subsidiaries, in compliance with family firms' preferences. The magnitude

Table 4.8 Probit models. Dependent variable: WOS. Sample: Combinations of performance hazard and emotional hazard

	(1)	*(2)*	*(3)*	*(4)*	*(5)*	*(6)*	*(7)*	*(8)*
	Low PH & High EH	Low PH & Low EH	High PH & High EH	High PH & Low EH	Low PH & High EH	Low PH & Low EH	High PH & High EH	High PH & Low EH
Family leader	**0.410****	-0.039	0.076	**-0.542*****	**0.369****	-0.050	0.056	**-0.534*****
	(0.134)	(0.251)	(0.442)	**(0.151)**	**(0.140)**	(0.250)	(0.434)	**(0.149)**
Cultural distance					0.291**	0.145†	0.424**	0.142**
					(0.098)	(0.086)	(0.150)	(0.051)
Family leader *x* Cultural distance					**-0.237***	-0.055	**-0.388***	0.052
					(0.119)	(0.103)	**(0.175)**	(0.069)
Parent age	0.002	0.007†	0.011	0.001	0.002	0.007†	0.012	0.001
	(0.004)	(0.004)	(0.013)	(0.003)	(0.004)	(0.004)	(0.013)	(0.003)
Parent size	0.271***	0.085	0.229	0.026	0.283***	0.081	0.220	0.028
	(0.072)	(0.077)	(0.199)	(0.038)	(0.074)	(0.076)	(0.198)	(0.039)
Leverage	0.070	-0.052*	0.026	0.012	0.073	-0.050*	0.021	0.013
	(0.050)	(0.024)	(0.044)	(0.010)	(0.053)	(0.023)	(0.043)	(0.010)
R&D intensity	12.021	-4.125	12.476	3.001	12.884	-3.653	13.786	3.233
	(13.328)	(8.413)	(23.168)	(3.389)	(13.213)	(8.500)	(23.068)	(3.240)
Family ownership	-0.130	0.095	0.361	0.411†	-0.089	0.179	0.350	0.430†
	(0.419)	(0.493)	(1.123)	(0.241)	(0.426)	(0.496)	(1.109)	(0.245)
First generation	0.373†	0.406†	0.105	0.112	0.368†	0.416†	0.131	0.108
	(0.200)	(0.212)	(0.565)	(0.126)	(0.202)	(0.213)	(0.550)	(0.127)
Female leader	-0.329	0.329	-0.635	-0.089	-0.311	0.378	-0.639	-0.125
	(0.273)	(0.476)	(0.498)	(0.193)	(0.280)	(0.477)	(0.500)	(0.190)
Tenure leader	-0.023**	-0.010	-0.000	0.001	-0.024**	-0.011	-0.002	0.002
	(0.008)	(0.011)	(0.024)	(0.007)	(0.008)	(0.011)	(0.023)	(0.007)
Country risk	-0.005	0.033†	0.005	0.004	-0.008	0.029	0.004	-0.000
	(0.023)	(0.019)	(0.026)	(0.014)	(0.023)	(0.019)	(0.026)	(0.015)

Administrative distance	0.008	-0.020	-0.075	-0.009	0.007	-0.022	-0.060	-0.020
	(0.049)	(0.037)	(0.133)	(0.038)	(0.049)	(0.036)	(0.131)	(0.038)
Geographic distance	-0.010	-0.013	-0.018	-0.004	-0.022	-0.023	-0.026	-0.022†
	(0.017)	(0.014)	(0.022)	(0.011)	(0.018)	(0.015)	(0.022)	(0.012)
Constant	-1.362†	-0.495	-2.255	-0.113	-1.349†	-0.529	-2.111	-0.101
	(0.696)	(0.872)	(1.890)	(0.490)	(0.702)	(0.873)	(1.869)	(0.501)
Industry dummies	Yes	Yes	Yes	Yes	Yes	Yes	Yes	Yes
Time dummies	Yes	Yes	Yes	Yes	Yes	Yes	Yes	Yes
Observations	535	936	572	1896	535	936	572	1896
Firms	56	148	119	263	56	148	119	263
Ratio of correct classification	81.44%	76.71%	72.79%	75.16%	81.05%	76.60%	73.47%	75.05%
Pseudo R^2	0.305	0.206	0.228	0.166	0.312	0.212	0.250	0.179
Likelihood ratio	165.30***	139.65***	52.72**	228.79***	169.50***	143.59***	58.29**	248.02***

Notes:

PH performance hazard, *EH* emotional hazard

Firm-level clustered standard errors in parentheses

†$p < 0.10$, *$p < 0.05$, **$p < 0.01$, ***$p < 0.001$

Pseudo R^2 follows the Cragg & Uhler's calculation

Table 4.9 Average marginal effects. Dependent variable: WOS. Sample: Combinations of performance hazard and emotional hazard

	(1)	*(2)*	*(3)*	*(4)*	*(5)*	*(6)*	*(7)*	*(8)*
	Low PH & High EH	Low PH & Low EH	High PH & High EH	High PH & Low EH	Low PH & High EH	Low PH & Low EH	High PH & High EH	High PH & Low EH
Family leader	**0.091****	-0.011	0.023	**-0.158*****	**0.082****	-0.014	0.017	**-0.154*****
	(0.030)	(0.068)	(0.136)	**(0.044)**	**(0.031)**	(0.068)	(0.131)	**(0.043)**
Cultural distance					0.065**	0.039†	0.128**	0.041**
					(0.021)	(0.023)	(0.045)	(0.015)
Family leader *x* Cultural distance					**-0.053***	-0.015	**-0.117***	0.015
					(0.026)	(0.028)	**(0.053)**	(0.020)
Parent age	0.000	0.002	0.004	0.000	0.000	0.002†	0.004	0.000
	(0.001)	(0.001)	(0.004)	(0.001)	(0.001)	(0.001)	(0.004)	(0.001)
Parent size	0.061***	0.023	0.071	0.008	0.063***	0.022	0.067	0.008
	(0.015)	(0.021)	(0.061)	(0.011)	(0.016)	(0.020)	(0.060)	(0.011)
Leverage	0.016	-0.014*	0.008	0.004	0.016	-0.013*	0.006	0.004
	(0.011)	(0.006)	(0.013)	(0.003)	(0.012)	(0.006)	(0.013)	(0.003)
R&D intensity	4.912†	-1.119	3.847	0.876	5.073†	-0.987	4.175	0.934
	(2.936)	(2.278)	(7.145)	(0.990)	(2.894)	(2.292)	(6.984)	(0.937)
Family ownership	-0.029	0.026	0.111	0.120†	-0.020	0.048	0.106	0.124†
	(0.094)	(0.134)	(0.345)	(0.070)	(0.095)	(0.134)	(0.335)	(0.070)
First generation	0.083†	0.110†	0.032	0.033	0.081†	0.112†	0.040	0.031
	(0.044)	(0.058)	(0.174)	(0.037)	(0.044)	(0.058)	(0.166)	(0.037)
Female leader	-0.073	0.089	-0.196	-0.026	-0.069	0.102	-0.193	-0.036
	(0.060)	(0.129)	(0.153)	(0.056)	(0.061)	(0.128)	(0.151)	(0.055)
Tenure leader	-0.005**	-0.003	-0.000	0.000	-0.005**	-0.003	-0.001	0.001
	(0.002)	(0.003)	(0.007)	(0.002)	(0.002)	(0.003)	(0.007)	(0.002)
Country risk	-0.001	0.009†	0.002	0.001	-0.002	0.008	0.001	-0.000

	(0.005)	(0.005)	(0.008)	(0.004)	(0.005)	(0.005)	(0.008)	(0.004)
Administrative distance	0.002	-0.005	-0.023	-0.003	0.002	-0.006	-0.018	-0.006
	(0.011)	(0.010)	(0.041)	(0.011)	(0.011)	(0.010)	(0.040)	(0.011)
Geographic distance	-0.002	-0.004	-0.006	-0.001	-0.005	-0.006	-0.008	-0.006†
	(0.004)	(0.004)	(0.007)	(0.003)	(0.004)	(0.004)	(0.007)	(0.004)
Industry dummies	Yes	Yes	Yes	Yes	Yes	Yes	Yes	Yes
Time dummies	Yes	Yes	Yes	Yes	Yes	Yes	Yes	Yes
Observations	535	936	572	1896	535	936	572	1896

Notes:

PH performance hazard, *EH* emotional hazard

Robust standard errors in parentheses

†$p < 0.10$, *$p < 0.05$, **$p < 0.01$, ***$p < 0.001$

of the effect is especially relevant for size, as one percent increase/ decrease leads to an increase/decrease of the probability of a wholly-owned subsidiary between 2.1 and 6.3 percent, across the sub-samples. The opposite is true for leverage. Coefficients—when significant—are always negative, meaning that more leveraged firms are less likely to establish a wholly-owned subsidiary. This is coherent with the expectation that leveraged firms face more difficulties to raise money to internationalize and thus they face financial constraints that leads to share the foreign venture with a partner. However, the magnitude is weak, as a unitary increase in leverage leads to roughly one percent decrease of wholly-owned subsidiary probability in the different sub-samples. Moreover, the coefficient of the first generation dummy is always positive, when significant. This effect can be explained by assuming that first generation family members show a tighter relationship with the family firm and, therefore, prefer avoiding establishing foreign subsidiaries with a partner. These firms are 5.1–11.2 percent more likely to establish a wholly-owned subsidiary than those held by family members of later generations.

From the last rows shown in Table 4.4, it emerges that the full sample consists of 3939 foreign entries run by 586 firms, an average of 6.72 foreign direct investments (FDIs) per firm. The same statistics for firms with high and low performance hazard are 7.21 and 6.46, respectively. This is coherent with the expectation that well performing firms have more resources to invest abroad and thus, they do it more often. The impact of the family leader in the full model is not significant and with negligible magnitude (the average marginal effect—not significant—is 1.1 percent). However, when we split the sample according to the performance hazard, such a weak effect is the result of a match between a positive (coef. = 0.426; *p*-value = 0.019) impact on wholly-owned subsidiary for those firms with low performance hazard and a negative one (coef. = -0.310; *p*-value = 0.015) for those with high performance hazard, as reported in models (4) and (6), respectively. Specifically, family leaders of firms with a low performance hazard showed a 10.7 percent higher probability of running a wholly-owned subsidiary than their non-family counterparts do. On the contrary, they lower such a probability by 9.5 percent when the firm have high performance hazard (see Table 4.5). This finding provides clear support for Proposition 1.

Focusing on emotional hazard, from Table 4.6 it is possible to observe that this type of hazard does not affect the proclivity to internationalize. Indeed, firms with high emotional hazard have an average foreign entry per firm of 6.34, whilst those with low emotional hazard reach a comparable value of 6.89. However, emotional hazard has a relevant effect for family leaders. Indeed, when emotional hazard is high, family leaders have a positive effect (coef. = 0.369; *p*-value = 0.011) on wholly-owned subsidiary preference, whilst the effect is negative for family leaders (coef. = -0.282; *p*-value = 0.020) when emotional hazard is low. In terms of average marginal effect, the presence of a family leader increases the probability of undertaking a wholly-owned subsidiary by 10.2 percent in family firms with high emotional hazard; such a probability is reduced by 8.6 percent when they lead firms with low emotional hazard (models (2) and (4) in Table 4.7).

The preceding findings are confirmed in Table 4.8. We have seen that the two types of hazard help in explaining the choice between wholly-owned subsidiary and joint venture. In particular, both low performance hazard and high emotional hazard push towards wholly-owned subsidiaries, while both high performance hazard and low emotional hazard lead to choose joint ventures. When the two hazards are combined, these effects strengthen or compensate each other. Family leaders have a strong and significant effect, with regard to wholly-owned subsidiary probability, in firms in low performance hazard and high emotional hazard (coef. = 0.410; *p*-value = 0.002), as reported in model (1) in Table 4.8. The effect of family leadership in terms of wholly-owned subsidiary probability is equal to a rise of 9.1 percent (model (1) in Table 4.9). The opposite is true for firms with high performance hazard and low emotional hazard (model (4) in Table 4.8). Namely, family leadership has a strong and negative effect for such firms (coef. = -0.542; *p*-value < 0.001). This leads to a reduction of the likelihood of choosing wholly-owned subsidiary of 15.8 percent. Models (2) and (3) of Table 4.8 show that, when firms have one hazard that push towards wholly-owned subsidiary and the other towards joint venture, the impact of the family leader is negligible and not significant. However, although they do not have enough statistical power, it is possible to note that the sign of the relationship always follows the emotional hazard driver, i.e. it is negative when emotional hazard is low, as in model (2), and it is positive when emotional hazard is high, as in model (3). Thus, Proposition 2 finds empirical support.

Finally, the role of cultural distance is investigated. In models (5) to (9) of Table 4.8, the cultural distance and its interaction with family leader are inserted. Cultural distance always has a positive sign in all the models, meaning that when cultural distance is high, firms in the sample are more likely to prefer entering the country with a wholly-owned subsidiary. The average marginal effects in Table 4.9 indicates that a one standard deviation increase/decrease in cultural distance augments (reduces) the wholly-owned subsidiary probability between 3.9 and 12.8 percent. Moving to the interaction effect, empirical evidence corroborates theoretical predictions of Proposition 3. Specifically, it was argued that cultural distance affects firms with high emotional hazard by reducing their propensity towards a wholly-owned subsidiary—i.e. reducing the willingness to hold the entire control of the foreign subsidiary—, whilst it should have a negligible effect on firms with low emotional hazard. Accordingly, the estimates show that when emotional hazard is high, models (5) and (7) of Table 4.8, the coefficients of the interaction terms are negative and significant. Namely, it is equal to -0.237 (p-value = 0.047) when the firm has also low performance hazard and it is -0.338 (p-value = 0.027) when the firm has high performance hazard. Average marginal effects are equal to -5.3 and -11.7 percent, respectively. On the other hand, when emotional hazard is low, coefficients have a smaller magnitude—in model (8), it is even slightly positive—and they are not significant. Consequently, average marginal effects are negligible (below 2 percent in absolute terms) and never significant.

4.5 Limitations

This study is not free from limitations. Theoretically, Chap. 3 proposes that the level of emotional hazard relies on the intensity of family identity. Firstly, whilst it is easy to agree that stronger family identity exposes family principals to higher emotional hazard, it is also true that the family identity may not be the only source of this type of hazard. Secondly, the direct effect of SEW preservation on the subsidiary performance is overlooked. This is an empirical issue, as the vast majority of subsidiaries do not report their financial data separately from the parent firm, thus making it hard to detect which is their performance after the foreign entry. Thirdly and most importantly, family leadership is considered as exogenous to the subsidiary ownership choice in line with previous studies on the topic (e.g. Brouthers & Hennart, 2007; Brouthers et al., 2003) also when considering other governance explanatory variable (Filatotchev et al., 2007). While this choice could be questioned, variables employed to instrument family leadership in the field such as the gender of the firstborn child (Bennedsen et al., 2010) might be related to the subsidiary ownership choice, proving to be a weak instrument in this case. Moreover, the several sample splits that characterize the structure of this analysis makes it hard to find a univocally stable instrument for all the regressions. Finally, despite theoretical arguments which inspire this analysis relates to family firms in general, data came only from Italian family firms. However, similarly to prior studies that relied on one-country data to investigate SEW logics in family business (e.g. Gomez-Mejia et al., 2007), findings can also be generalizable for family firms in other countries.

4.6 Contribution to Theory and Practice

For the purpose of investigating the SEW's theoretical foundations and the antecedents of decision-makers behaviors, the empirical evidence provided helps to better understand logics underlying family leaders' strategic decision-making in front of a particularly relevant decision during the internationalization process: the subsidiary ownership choice. Specifically, by taking into consideration how the family leaders' aversion to lose family control varies depends on the given circumstances, this chapter challenges the universalistic assumption that SEW preservation is a vaguely emotional decision-making criterion for family leaders (Berrone et al., 2010; Gomez-Mejia et al., 2007). Together with the conceptual investigation in Chap. 3, the analysis provides support for the idea that both performance hazard and emotional hazard might influence the emphasis that family leaders place on SEW preservation and consequently, how strong their family control loss aversion is in strategic decision-making. Additionally, by considering the role of cultural distance between the domestic and the host country (which is particularly relevant for subsidiary ownership policies), it detects a specific foreign context-related issue that may shape the family leader's emotional decision-making driver.

In more detail, the empirical investigation on a sample of 3939 subsidiary ownership policies run by 586 family firms shows that when the family firm is suffering low performance (i.e. exposed to high performance hazard), the family leader is less focused on avoiding family control losses, preferring foreign investments shared with an external partner (namely, joint venture). This strategic approach switches to the opposite when the family leader operates in a well-performing firm (i.e. exposed to low performance hazard) as family leaders are more likely to establish a wholly-owned subsidiary. Secondly, the above tendency appears moderated by the level of emotional hazard. The findings show that family leaders have a stronger positive relation with a wholly-owned subsidiary when low level of performance hazard couples with high levels of emotional hazard, i.e. when there is a strong family identity due to identical family and company names (Zellweger et al., 2010, 2013). Conversely, family leaders have a stronger negative relation with wholly-owned subsidiaries (thus more likely to choose joint ventures) when high level of performance hazard couples with less emotional hazard. That supports the idea that family leader's strategic behavior is driven by emotional components only *when* economic conditions of the firm permit so (Gomez-Mejia et al., 2018; Calabrò et al., 2018). As such, *this study provides a less "emotional" interpretation of SEW, showing that the choice to give priority to emotions is deliberate, situational, and pertained to those family firms exhibiting a high level of family identity.*

Hence, this study contributes to the body of studies on family firms internationalization by investigating the role of family control loss aversion—stemming from the main goal of SEW preservation—in driving family leaders' entry mode decisions (e.g. Boellis et al., 2016; Hennart & Slangen, 2014; Pongelli et al., 2016, 2021; Xu et al., 2020). The empirical analyses—along with the theoretical investigation included in Chap. 3—confirm and expand the notion that the loss aversion for family leaders has a different intensity depending on certain circumstances (Gomez-Mejia et al., 2010, 2018). Indeed, findings show that family leader's strategic preferences towards the subsidiary ownership choice substantially vary based on how those circumstances occur. In doing so, this chapter contributes to a deeper understanding of behavioral theories specifically in the context of family decision-makers, by providing evidence that the family leader's loss aversion is either strengthened or weakened depending on the level of performance hazard, emotional hazard and cultural distance, with subsequently different strategic choices. Altogether, the results give a comprehensive picture about the determinants of strategic decision-making in family firms, providing a more articulated interpretation of the "emotional" component of SEW.

Additionally, with respect to the moderating role of cultural distance, this chapter suggests that moving from the domestic to the foreign context the SEW preservation goal might be subjected to change. As cultural distance increases, family leaders are more likely to choose joint ventures and therefore are more willing to dilute family control and threatening SEW preservation: this result is robust even under high emotional hazard and regardless of the level of performance hazard (Fig. 4.1). In culturally

	High performance hazard	Low performance hazard
High emotional hazard	**n.s.** (High cultural distance: **Joint venture**)	**Wholly-owned subsidiary** (High cultural distance: **Joint venture**)
Low emotional hazard	**Joint venture** (High cultural distance: **n.s.**)	**n.s.** (High cultural distance: **n.s**)

Fig. 4.1 Results of the analyses

distant countries, family control loss aversion seems to be no more the primary reference point for strategic decision-making. As such, this study contributes to the lively debate on the role of cultural distance for the subsidiary ownership choice which is mainly inconclusive so far due to the mixed empirical evidence (e.g. Chang & Rosenzweig, 2001; Luo, 2001). In the attempt to bridge the international business and the family business literatures, this chapter represents one of the first efforts to pinpoint cultural distance as a particularly relevant factor for the risk assessment of the subsidiary ownership choice in the specific context of family firms and introduces the idea that cultural distance is an external contingency that push family leaders to revise the family firm's international strategic agenda (Beugelsdijk et al., 2018; López-Duarte & Vidal-Suárez, 2010; Shenkar, 2001).

The theoretical and empirical findings of this research also have implications for practice. Indeed, they shed light on the emotional ingredient of the family leader's strategic decision-making which arise from the overlapping between the family and the business, and it is particularly visible in family firms which carry the family name. Although it is still controversial the extent to which it could be an advantage or rather a disadvantage, is argued that the family owners should meditate on this issue.

The awareness of the role socioemotional factors might have on the subsidiary ownership choice could help family decision-makers consider in advance the controversial effects of their emotional attachment on the firm. To make the best decisions in overseas markets and to assess objectively the advantages and threats of each subsidiary ownership choice, they could benefit from the counseling and advisory role of external advisors with a set of specific international competence, and who could help family firms objectively evaluate the benefits and risk associated with subsidiary ownership choices.

References

Amore, M. D., Garofalo, O., & Minichilli, A. (2014). Gender interactions within the family firm. *Management Science, 60*(5), 1083–1097. https://doi.org/10.1287/mnsc.2013.1824

Anderson, R. C., & Reeb, D. M. (2003). Founding-family ownership and firm performance: Evidence from the S&P 500. *The Journal of Finance, 58*(3), 1301–1328. https://doi.org/10.1111/1540-6261.00567

Avloniti, A., & Filippaios, F. (2014). Unbundling the differences between psychic and cultural distance: An empirical examination of the existing measures. *International Business Review, 23*(3), 660–674. https://doi.org/10.1016/j.ibusrev.2013.11.007

Banalieva, E. R., & Eddleston, K. A. (2011). Home-region focus and performance of family firms: The role of family vs non-family leaders. *Journal of International Business Studies, 42*(8), 1060–1072. https://doi.org/10.1057/jibs.2011.28

Bennedsen, M., Pérez-González, F., & Wolfenzon, D. (2010). The governance of family firms. In K. Baker & R. Anderson (Eds.), *Corporate Governance: A Synthesis of Theory, Research, and Practice* (pp. 371–389). John Wiley & Sons.

Berrone, P., Cruz, C., Gomez-Mejia, L. R., & Larraza-Kintana, M. (2010). Socioemotional wealth and corporate responses to institutional pressures: Do family-controlled firms pollute less? *Administrative Science Quarterly, 55*(1), 82–113. https://doi.org/10.2189/asqu.2010.55.1.82

Berry, H., Guillen, M. F., & Zhou, N. (2010). An institutional approach to cross-national distance. *Journal of International Business Studies, 41*(9), 1460–1480. https://doi.org/10.1057/jibs.2010.28

Beugelsdijk, S., Kostova, T., Kunst, V. E., Spadafora, E., & Van Essen, M. (2018). Cultural distance and firm internationalization: A meta-analytical review and theoretical implications. *Journal of Management, 44*(1), 89–130. https://doi.org/10.1177/0149206317729027

Boellis, A., Mariotti, S., Minichilli, A., & Piscitello, L. (2016). Family involvement and firms' establishment mode choice in foreign markets. *Journal of International Business Studies, 47*(8), 929–950. https://doi.org/10.1057/jibs.2016.23

Brouthers, K. D. (2002). Institutional, cultural and transaction cost influences on entry mode choice and performance. *Journal of International Business Studies, 33*(2), 203–221. https://doi.org/10.1057/palgrave.jibs.8491013

Brouthers, K. D., & Hennart, J. F. (2007). Boundaries of the firm: Insights from international entry mode research. *Journal of Management, 33*(3), 395–425. https://doi.org/10.1177/0149206307300817

Brouthers, K. D., Brouthers, L. E., & Werner, S. (2003). Transaction cost-enhanced entry mode choices and firm performance. *Strategic Management Journal, 24*(12), 1239–1248. https://doi.org/10.1002/smj.362

Calabrò, A., Minichilli, A., Amore, M. D., & Brogi, M. (2018). The courage to choose! Primogeniture and leadership succession in family firms. *Strategic Management Journal, 39*(7), 2014–2035. https://doi.org/10.1002/smj.2760

Cameron, A. C., & Trivedi, P. K. (2005). *Microeconometrics: Methods and applications.* Cambridge University Press.

Chang, S. J., & Rosenzweig, P. M. (2001). The choice of entry mode in sequential foreign direct investment. *Strategic Management Journal, 22*(8), 747–776. https://doi.org/10.1002/smj.168

Cho, K. R., & Padmanabhan, P. (1995). Acquisition versus new venture: The choice of foreign establishment mode by Japanese firms. *Journal of International Management, 1*(3), 255–285.

De Maesschalck, R., Jouan-Rimbaud, D., & Massart, D. L. (2000). The mahalanobis distance. *Chemometrics and Intelligent Laboratory Systems, 50*(1), 1–18. https://doi.org/10.1016/S0169-7439(99)00047-7

Faccio, M., & Lang, L. H. (2002). The ultimate ownership of Western European corporations. *Journal of Financial Economics, 65*(3), 365–395. https://doi.org/10.1016/S0304-405X(02)00146-0

Filatotchev, I., Strange, R., Piesse, J., & Lien, Y. C. (2007). FDI by firms from newly industrialised economies in emerging markets: Corporate governance, entry mode and location. *Journal of International Business Studies, 38*(4), 556–572. https://doi.org/10.1057/palgrave.jibs.8400279

Gomez-Mejia, L. R., Haynes, K. T., Núñez-Nickel, M., Jacobson, K. J., & Moyano-Fuentes, J. (2007). Socioemotional wealth and business risks in family-controlled firms: Evidence from Spanish olive oil mills. *Administrative Science Quarterly, 52*(1), 106–137. https://doi.org/10.2189/asqu.52.1.106

Gomez-Mejia, L. R., Makri, M., & Larraza-Kintana, M. (2010). Diversification decisions in family-controlled firms. *Journal of Management Studies, 47*(2), 223–252. https://doi.org/10.1111/j.1467-6486.2009.00889.x

Gomez-Mejia, L. R., Patel, P. C., & Zellweger, T. M. (2018). In the horns of the dilemma: Socioemotional wealth, financial wealth, and acquisitions in family firms. *Journal of Management, 44*(4), 1369–1397. https://doi.org/10.1177/0149206315614375

Hair, J. F., Black, W. C., Babin, B. J., & Anderson, R. E. (2009). *Multivariate data analysis: A global perspective* (7th ed.). Prentice Hall.

Hennart, J. F., & Reddy, S. (1997). The choice between mergers/acquisitions and joint ventures: The case of Japanese investors in the United States. *Strategic*

Management Journal, 18(1), 1–12. https://doi.org/10.1002/(SICI)1097-0266(199701)18:1<1::AID-SMJ862>3.0.CO;2-R

Hennart, J. F., & Slangen, A. H. (2014). Yes, we really do need more entry mode studies! A commentary on Shaver. *Journal of International Business Studies, 46*(1), 114–122. https://doi.org/10.1057/jibs.2014.39

Hennart, J. F., Sheng, H. H., & Pimenta, G. (2015). Local complementary inputs as drivers of entry mode choices: The case of US investments in Brazil. *International Business Review, 24*(3), 466–475. https://doi.org/10.1016/j.ibusrev.2014.10.005

Hofstede, G. (1980). *Culture's consequences: International differences in work related values.* Sage.

Inglehart, R. (2004). *Human beliefs and values.* Siglo XXI.

La Porta, R., Lopez de Silanes, F., & Shleifer, A. (1999). Corporate ownership around the world. *The Journal of Finance, 54*(2), 471–517. https://doi.org/10.1111/0022-1082.00115

Leary, M. T., & Roberts, M. R. (2014). Do peer firms affect corporate financial policy? *The Journal of Finance, 69*(1), 139–178. https://doi.org/10.1111/jofi.12094

López-Duarte, C., & Vidal-Suárez, M. M. (2010). External uncertainty and entry mode choice: Cultural distance, political risk and language diversity. *International Business Review, 19*(6), 575–588. https://doi.org/10.1016/j.ibusrev.2010.03.007

Luo, Y. (2001). Determinants of entry in an emerging economy: A multilevel approach. *Journal of Management Studies, 38*(3), 443–472. https://doi.org/10.1111/1467-6486.00244

Makino, S., & Neupert, K. E. (2000). National culture, transaction costs, and the choice between joint venture and wholly owned subsidiary. *Journal of International Business Studies, 31*(4), 705–713. https://doi.org/10.1057/palgrave.jibs.8490930

Mariotti, S., Mutinelli, M., & Sansoucy, L. (2015). *Italia multinazionale 2014: Le partecipazioni italiane all'estero ed estere in Italia.* Rubbettino Editore.

Miller, D., Le Breton-Miller, I., & Lester, R. H. (2010). Family ownership and acquisition behavior in publicly-traded companies. *Strategic Management Journal, 31*(2), 201–223. https://doi.org/10.1002/smj.802

Miller, D., Minichilli, A., & Corbetta, G. (2013). Is family leadership always beneficial? *Strategic Management Journal, 34*(5), 553–571. https://doi.org/10.1002/smj.2024

Minichilli, A., Brogi, M., & Calabrò, A. (2016). Weathering the storm: Family ownership, governance, and performance through the financial and economic crisis. *Corporate Governance: An International Review, 24*(6), 552–568. https://doi.org/10.1111/corg.12125

OECD. (2015). *Country risk classification.*

Padmanabhan, P., & Cho, K. R. (1996). Ownership strategy for a foreign affiliate: An empirical investigation of Japanese firms. *Management International Review, 36*(1), 45–65.

Pongelli, C., Caroli, M. G., & Cucculelli, M. (2016). Family business going abroad: The effect of family ownership on foreign market entry mode decisions. *Small Business Economics, 47*(3), 787–801. https://doi.org/10.1007/s11187-016-9763-4

Pongelli, C., Calabrò, A., Quarato, F., Minichilli, A., & Corbetta, G. (2021). Out of the comfort zone! Family leaders' subsidiary ownership choices and the role of vulnerabilities. *Family Business Review, 34*(4), 404–424. https://doi.org/10.1177/08944865211050858

Sciascia, S., Mazzola, P., Astrachan, J. H., & Pieper, T. M. (2012). The role of family ownership in international entrepreneurship: Exploring nonlinear effects. *Small Business Economics, 38*(1), 15–31. https://doi.org/10.1007/s11187-010-9264-9

Shenkar, O. (2001). Cultural distance revisited: Towards a more rigorous conceptualization and measurement of cultural differences. *Journal of International Business Studies, 32*(3), 519–535. https://doi.org/10.1057/palgrave.jibs.8490982

Strike, V. M., Berrone, P., Sapp, S. G., & Congiu, L. (2015). A socioemotional wealth approach to CEO career horizons in family firms. *Journal of Management Studies, 52*(4), 555–583. https://doi.org/10.1111/joms.12123

Xu, K., Hitt, M. A., & Miller, S. R. (2020). The ownership structure contingency in the sequential international entry mode decision process: Family owners and institutional investors in family-dominant versus family-influenced firms. *Journal of International Business Studies, 51*(2), 151–171. https://doi.org/10.1057/s41267-019-00250-8

Zahra, S. A. (2003). International expansion of US manufacturing family businesses: The effect of ownership and involvement. *Journal of Business Venturing, 18*(4), 495–512. https://doi.org/10.1016/S0883-9026(03)00057-0

Zellweger, T. M., Eddleston, K. A., & Kellermanns, F. W. (2010). Exploring the concept of familiness: Introducing family firm identity. *Journal of Family Business Strategy, 1*(1), 54–63. https://doi.org/10.1016/j.jfbs.2009.12.003

Zellweger, T. M., Nason, R. S., Nordqvist, M., & Brush, C. G. (2013). Why do family firms strive for nonfinancial goals? An organizational identity perspective. *Entrepreneurship Theory and Practice, 37*(2), 229–248. https://doi.org/10.1111/j.1540-6520.2011.00466

Index[1]

A
Acquisition, 22–24, 37, 42, 59

B
Behavioral agency model (BAM), 48
Bifurcation bias, 14
Board of directors, 14, 15, 18, 24, 36, 57

C
Contractual agreement, 10, 12, 16–17
Cooperation, 10, 12, 16, 47
Corporate governance, 12, 15, 56
Cultural distance, 5, 6, 39, 41, 45–49, 45n1, 56, 57, 60, 61, 67n3, 77–81
Culture, 15, 46, 47, 57

E
Emotional hazard, 5, 6, 38, 39, 41, 43–45, 47–49, 56, 61, 65, 66, 67n1, 70–80
Equity modes, 10, 12
Establishment mode, 12, 23
Export, 4, 10–18, 20

F
Familiness, 11, 17
Family CEO, 14, 19, 37
Family control, 2, 3, 5, 6, 14, 19, 36–38, 40–45, 47, 48, 63, 65, 79–81
Family involvement, 13, 15, 16, 20–24, 36, 39, 63
Family leader, 5, 6, 14, 22, 38, 40–48, 57, 59, 61, 65–67, 67n1, 67n2, 67n3, 76, 77, 79–81

[1] Note: Page numbers followed by 'n' refer to notes.

C. Pongelli, *Family Firms into International Markets*,
https://doi.org/10.1007/978-3-031-05398-6

Foreign direct investments (FDI), 11, 17–21, 23, 41, 56, 76
Foreign subsidiaries, 6, 11, 18–21, 23, 37, 41, 49, 57, 76, 78
Franchising, 10, 16, 17

G
Generation, 15, 24, 59, 63, 67n3, 76
Goals, 2, 5, 15, 16, 22, 23, 36, 37, 40, 42–44, 48, 80
Greenfield investment, 22–24, 37

I
Identity, 3n2, 43, 44, 47, 48, 65–67, 78, 80

J
Joint venture, 4–6, 10–12, 16, 21–22, 36–49, 56–82

L
Literature review, 4

M
Multinationality, 17, 18

N
Non-equity modes, 10, 12

O
Ownership, 3, 5, 6, 12–15, 17–21, 23, 24, 36–40, 45, 48, 49, 56, 58–61, 67n3, 79

P
Performance, 4–6, 12–14, 16, 17, 19, 37–39, 41, 42, 48, 49, 56, 61, 65–67, 78, 79
Performance hazard, 5, 6, 37, 38, 41–45, 47–49, 56, 61, 65–69, 67n1, 72–80

Q
Qualitative studies, 11, 16

R
Reputation, 16, 21, 36, 43, 44, 47
Risk preferences, 3, 3n2, 5, 16, 24, 37, 38, 47, 48

S
Sequential approach, 11, 12
Socioemotional wealth (SEW), 3, 3n2, 5, 13, 16, 23, 36–49, 66, 78–80
Subsidiary ownership choice, 5, 12, 21, 22, 38, 43, 49, 78–82

W
Wholly owned subsidiary, 5, 6, 10, 12, 16, 21–22, 36–49, 56–82

FSC
www.fsc.org
MIX
Papier | Fördert
gute Waldnutzung
FSC® C083411

Kolibri 360 GmbH
Ferdinand-Jühlke-Straße 7
99095 Erfurt, Deutschland
produktsicherheit@kolibri360.de